Foreword
DR. FRANCES ANN BAILEY

BREAK THE CHAINS

LIBERATING YOUR LINEAGE FROM GENERATIONAL CURSES

Visionary Author
DR. LASHONDA WOFFORD

Studio Griffin
A Publishing Company
www.studiogriffin.net

Breaking The Chains: Liberating Your Lineage From Generational Curses. Copyright © 2024. Dr. Lashonda Wofford.

All Rights Reserved. Printed in the United States of America.
No part of this book may be used or reproduced in any manner whatsoever without written permission except in the case of brief quotations embodied in critical articles and reviews.

For information, contact:
Studio Griffin
A Publishing Company
studiogriffin@outlook.com
www.studiogriffin.net

Cover Design by Ruth E. Griffin
Images by © rawpixel.com and sea and sun/Adobe
Photos © Dr. Lashonda Wofford

All scripture quotations taken from The Holy Bible, King James Version, public domain.

First Edition

ISBN-13: 978-1-954818-48-4

Library of Congress Control Number: 2024913262

1 2 3 4 5 6 7 8 9 10

This book is lovingly dedicated to the grandparents, parents, children, and the generations yet to come. Through your enduring strength and relentless hope, you have given us the courage to face and break the chains that have weighed down our family for far too long.

To our ancestors who faced hardships we can only imagine, to our parents who began the formidable task of untying the knots of the past, and to our children, the bearers of our hopes and dreams for a future unshackled from the burdens we once carried—this is for you.

As we pen these pages, we vow to continue the work you started. We commit to being diligent and intentional, ensuring that the shadows of generational trauma, poverty, and dysfunction do not darken the lives of our descendants. We strive to create a legacy of healing, prosperity, and emotional freedom, so that those who follow may live their lives to the fullest, liberated from the past and hopeful for the future.

Thank you for your sacrifices, your prayers, and your undying belief in liberation and transformation. May this book serve as a testament to our collective journey towards breaking free, a journey we boldly continue in your honor.

Love Always & Forever,

The Chain Breakers

CONTENTS

Foreword: Chain Breaker   1
Dr. Frances Ann Bailey

Chapter 1: Unveiling the Legacy   5
Willie McCrimmon Jr.

Chapter 2: The Anatomy of Curses   17
Dr. Rashia N. Barbee

Chapter 3. Healing Through Awareness   29
ShaQuandra Dawson

Chapter 4: Rewriting Family Narratives   40
Travis Wofford

Chapter 5: The Path to Forgiveness   56
Dawanna Alexander

Chapter 6: Traditions of Release   69
Nichole Shoffner

Chapter 7: Intergenerational Healing   89
Shani'ya Faucette

Chapter 8: Embracing Positive Change   102
Dr. Karon Graves

Chapter 9: Guarding Against Recurrence   117
Dr. Lashonda Wofford

Acknowledgements   155

About the Authors   157

FOREWORD
Chain Breaker
Dr. Frances Ann Bailey

A generational curse breaker is handpicked by God to be the one who stands up and says, "It stops here!" Are you the one? Are you tired of seeing things in your family passed down that don't produce good fruit? Sick and tired of settling for the average in your bloodline? If you answer "Yes!", this book will give you the blueprint to break the chains over your bloodline and rise as a generational curse breaker. I challenge you to become the one, the handpicked vessel, the misunderstood advocate, the C.H.A.I.N. B.R.E.A.K.E.R.

Continues to press forward despite opposition. Conflict may arise but the compassion to see another free overrides the inner voice that says to quit. Knowing the why behind the bondage gives a thrust of boldness that something has to change and that nothing changes if nothing changes.

Holds onto the promise of God that before 'I formed you in your mother's womb, I already knew you.' (Jeremiah 1:5) So, if God has called you to be the one, you know that he has already groomed you for now. You have what it takes to breakthrough for your bloodline. The Chain Breaker helps others see what has been keeping them bound. They speak the truth in love and kindness that bring about repentance.

Agrees that you have to participate in your own deliverance if your deliverance requires a process; and obey the call to be the Moses of the family. See, a lot of times, we think because we are the Chain Breaker, we don't need deliverance, but the deliverer needs constant deliverance. Walking through deliverance allows you to be an effective Chain Breaker.

Insist on pleasing God and not people. Being a Chain Breaker can require you to walk a lonely, misunderstood road, but the breaker understands not being understood. They know without faith it is impossible to please God, so they answer the call and walk boldly in it. They understand that not everyone in the family will understand why they won't just deal with the abnormal or accept the normal. They create a lane of difference in a room full of those emulating each other.

Never compromise to prove a point or compromise God's word. A Chain Breaker lives a life that preaches they don't have to become like those they are trying to help deliver and set free. Chain Breakers maintain their character and integrity even while trying to set another free or share sound doctrine.

Believe in yourself. Chain Breakers are confident in the God in them to break curses. They work to protect their self-esteem and constantly stay before the Lord, seeking to see themselves the way he sees them. They don't let others tell them who they want them to be, rather they have an authentic identity in God.

Repent when needed. Chain Breakers never allow pride to lead them to destruction. They walk with a spirit of repentance and change their minds about things they could do differently. Change starts initially with you, so Chain Breakers are accountable to themselves first before trying to hold others accountable.

Evaluate situations and respond with the fruits of the Spirit. As a Chain Breaker, you should exhibit the fruits of the Spirit when you witness. The fruits of the Spirit are love, joy, peace, forbearance, kindness, goodness, faithfulness, gentleness, and self-control.

Allow the Holy Spirit to be the foundation of deliverance. As a Chain Breaker, we realize that we do not have to perform rituals to break bondage off of our life. Chain Breakers do not open the door that allows satanic activity to become a part of their lives by doing things such as rituals to cleanse themselves. Chain Breakers understand that God is God alone and nothing should try to perform the job of the Holy Spirit.

Keep God's commandments. Chain Breakers understand the importance of staying in God's will and not following emotions. Chain Breakers are mature in their emotions and understand that their hearts can lie to them. They test their emotions and motives with the Word of God and act accordingly.

Escapes the snare. Chain Breakers do not fear man, but they trust in the Lord. They will not succumb to word curses released by those who don't understand their assignment. They cast down all imaginations that exalt themselves against the Word of God and walk with the mind of God.

Remember who goes before them. Chain Breakers know that if God is for them, then no can be against them. They don't open doors to fears that restrict them or hold them back. They speak the Word of God and allow it to be the lamp to their feet.

Chain Breakers are equipped mentally, emotionally, and physically to go forth with the assignment God has for them. Stand up today and become one. Your family needs you.

CHAPTER 1
Unveiling The Legacy
Willie McCrimmon, Jr.

As the world shifts and the things we know begin to change right before our eyes, the one thing we often feel is the hunger to know more, want more and to feel complete within ourselves. That desire for some is now standing out like never before. The longing for greater, the fighting for purpose, and the asking about one's destiny has now started to resonate with many across the globe. Most of us have questioned our ability to achieve or the lack thereof; and we have wondered why the struggles have been so hard. It has gone beyond our private and internal thinking to become a part of our everyday conversations. Within the most inner part of our circles, we have conversed and realized that there have been roads traveled throughout life that for some were much harder and more severe than others. With thoughts formulating daily and taking assessments of our lives, it's easy to sit back and ask the questions, why have we not achieved the heights and the depths of our giftings and callings? Why haven't we accomplished the visions and plans that were once so adequately laid out before us? Where did we go wrong? Did someone or something put us in the wrong place? Did someone release and or speak ill concerning you and me? Or are we on the right path in general?

This and other things could simply be an assumption brought on by a mental state of confusion due to one's own paranoia. Where you are spiritually and what you believe, might determine the answers you may receive. We must understand that these and other questions often go unanswered, leaving many baffled and confused about the suffering and mistreatment of life.

Often, we carry the feelings of familiarity when it comes to the battles we've faced in our past and the circumstances we are currently dealing with into our now. Without restraint, our problems continue to be a part of the same makeup. It's typically the same attacks, the same warfare, and the same issues at hand. They all become repetitive, having similar origins with commonly known devices from the attack. It is a selective group of people. A people with certain places of recurring events that somehow continue to keep us bound. It feels as if an unforeseen force fights from the dark shadows of our lives, making things more difficult, harsh, and harder than we could imagine.

If this is the case, then what is this battle that is constantly fought but not always seen? What is this lurking around and found in every corner of our lives? Destructive to us but never visible to others? The faces of this added warfare may differ from time- to- time and the scenery may even change, but the assignment to fight our progress remains the same.

For many, the feeling of slow-paced movement and constant struggles, coupled with the reality of not being able to move forward, conquer, and establish looks more like a small window of hope mixed in with a condensed and complicated dream. The placement into broken positions throughout our lives with no real answers on why has even the greatest of us hurt, upset, and dumbfounded about our reoccurring outcomes. The knowledge earned throughout our lives along with our passion for life should have gotten us further than our current situations and circumstances but that hasn't always been the case and now the masses want to know why.

Too many know the battle with and have felt the continued fight from the stagnation of small towns, small minds, and even smaller outcomes. As many take a deeper look, they can now see that deepening mark on their progress. With this influence and unadjusted mindset, it is easy to see how the effects follow us from season-to-season, situation-to-situation and person-to-person year after year. Instead of properly maneuvering spiritually, we reluctantly try to press on only to find out that in life people have found themselves at a standstill. This burdensome feeling has had all of us perplexed at one point or another and often in deep thought about the root of it all. Flustered and frustrated, the question comes up again. What is this battle, this fight, that we find ourselves in? Well, my friends there is a name behind it all and it's narrowed down to two words:

Generational Curses

Generational curses bring broken scenarios, unresolved bouts of failure, the mentality of wrong thinking, and irregular actions that often cause irrevocable harm to the person and persons attached to him or her. It could be a plethora of negative things that are passed down from generation-to-generation and bloodline-to-bloodline. This mindset breeds corrupted patterns and behaviors that are the causes of never-ending tussles of lack, cloudy to no vision, constant and consistent issues of establishment, the repeating of broken cycles and for some, the lack of ability to follow God's words and His teachings.

What happened? How did this start and how can it end? These are formidable questions that have begun to resonate louder and louder in the lives of the spiritually desperate as well as those just trying to make it. The knowledgeable, gifted, and intelligent have found themselves wounded from these effects. The downtrodden are all wondering why there are reoccurring outcomes happening in their lives. Even the anointed have had seasons where they too have felt stuck in an endless cycle of despair.

These, along with many other questions, are at the forefront of our psyche and we will try to shine a light on and attempt to address some of the scenarios within this book. From the silent problems that continue to lurk behind the scenes of some of our most demonstrative fights to the ability to fight through and beyond the pain of it all. We must prevail. As we continue to grow spiritually, we now see that some of the biggest issues that are prevalent in the lives of many are also some of the same recurring strongholds that have paralyzed believers worldwide.

Yes, Generational Curses.

First, what is a curse? And what is a curse as we might know it today? According to Merriam-Webster(.com), the definition of a curse is:

- A prayer or invocation for harm or injury to come upon one
- A profane or obscene oath or word
- Something that is cursed or accursed
- Evil or misfortune that comes as if in response to imprecation or as retribution
- A cause of great harm or misfortune

It is the thing that has caused and contaminated good works, great intentions, and purpose driven foundations to be reduced to nothingness. When dealing with or in a curse, it can cause the fights to stay afloat; they are harder, more frequent, and even suffer and there only seem to be few that know the difference or the meaning why. The Apostle Paul said it best, when he stated, "When I would do good evil is present with me (Romans 7:21)." That statement alone has spoken volumes to the masses. Those wondering what happened within their life and what may have caused this added warfare and turmoil. constant struggles, and setback after setback. For some curses especially generational curses have been the known author of mismanaging people, time, places, and things.

It would have been easier for us to battle this thing if it had a specific face or was more open and visible to the naked eye. It would have been something to hit in prayer had we known or had the proper knowledge and wherewithal to learn, assess, and apply. Now we must combat this way of life while we can and address it through modern techniques of teaching and applicable means of strategically sound warfare. We must understand that with such a massive stronghold and defining spiritual grip, this opponent has not relinquished its hold on believers and the world alike.

There are several types of curses found in the Bible as well as those that have been affiliated in other religions, beliefs, and practices. The origin varies from bloodline to bloodline or person to person but as believers of Jesus Christ and the word of God, we know the origin of Generational Curses started in the third chapter of the book of Genesis. We could write several books on this topic but here are a few curses that may be familiar and their scripture references for how they started and how they operate.

Word Curses	James 3:1-12 Numbers 30:2 Romans 12:14 Proverbs 12:13-14 Galatians 3:15 Jonah 2:9
Disobedience	Hebrews 10:26-31 Galatians 3:10 Psalms 81:15 Daniel 9:11 Revelation 22:7 Jeremiah 11:3
Possessing cursed items	Deuteronomy 7:25 Joshua 6:18 Acts 19:19
Those who practice sorcery	Revelation 22:15 1 Samuel 15:23

	Leviticus 19:26
Rebellious kids	2 Timothy 3:2-9
	Deuteronomy 21:18-21
Idolatry	Jeremiah 44:8
	Exodus 22:20
	James 5:12
The house of the wicked	Proverbs 3:33
Swearing falsely	Zechariah 5:3-4
Thieves	Proverbs 15:27
Adding/taking from the word of God	Revelation 22:18-19
	Galatians 1:6-10
Death of the unborn	Exodus 21:22-23
False Prophets	Deuteronomy 18:20-22
	Ezekiel 33:30
	Jeremiah 23
Those who curse their rulers	Exodus 22:28
	Romans 13:1-5
	Acts 23:5
	Ecclesiastes 10:20
Idolatry	Jeremiah 44:8
	Psalms 81:15
	Matthew 5:34-37
	Revelation 9:20-21

There are five types of curses within the list that constantly have a main theme:

- Word Curses
- Self-Pronounced Curses
- Curses from God
- Curses sent from occultic means
- Generational Curses

The parts of the curse that we must focus on are not the actions and results that take place from the curse but the thinking and perspective that one operates in while dealing in the curse.

The wrong thinking, the wrong perspective, and the wrong vantage point will always produce the wrong fruit within one's life. So again, the strongest part of a generational curse that we might be fighting against is not necessarily the actions committed but the decision and mindset that one walks in. Actions can typically heal faster than a broken mindset. The Bible declares in Matthew 15:19-20, *"For out of the heart proceed evil thoughts, murders, adulteries, fornications, thefts, false witness, blasphemies: These are the things which defile a man."*

So, what indicates dirtiness, uncleanliness or being foul is not the action of what we do but the intent, perspective, and view of what is done. Generational curses and curses are broken mindsets that never change, no matter how hard the situation may be for generations! The curse is a broken mindset that continues to breed dysfunction with hardly any help of escape! It's saddening me to say that many of us are operating from a place of dysfunction, a broken mindset, and warped perspective. So many love God, choose God, worship God and desire to walk in a life that's pleasing to God but have dysfunctional and tampered mindsets that have been passed down through the family and will often cause chaos and despair for years to come.

Generational Curses are often talked about but never understood with how they touch our lives. We have all been influenced knowingly or unknowingly by what runs in our bloodline. Cain dealt with it, David dealt with it, Isaac dealt with it, and the list goes on and on. We must acknowledge the pattern that we see in us, the sin that is reoccurring around us, and transition our mind from what we've known to the real word of God and deliverance for us because if not we will remain trapped in and endless cycle of despair and having to battle with the dangers of the repercussions found in Deuteronomy 28:15-68:

But it shall come to pass, if thou wilt not hearken unto the voice of the LORD thy God, to observe to do all his commandments and his statutes which I command thee this day; that all these curses shall come upon thee, and overtake thee: cursed shalt thou be in the city, and cursed shalt thou be in the field. Cursed shall be thy basket and thy store. Cursed shall be the fruit of thy body, and the fruit of thy land, the increase of thy kind, and the flocks of thy sheep. Cursed shalt thou be when thou comest in, and cursed shalt thou be when thou goest out. The LORD shall send upon thee cursing, vexation, and rebuke, in all that thou settest thine hand unto for to do, until thou be destroyed, and until thou perish quickly; because of the wickedness of thy doings, whereby thou hast forsaken me. The LORD shall make the pestilence cleave unto thee, until he have consumed thee from off the land, whither thou goest to possess it. The LORD shall smite thee with a consumption, and with a fever, and with an inflammation, and with an extreme burning, and with the sword, and with blasting, and with mildew; and they shall pursue thee until thou perish. And thy heaven that is over thy head shall be brass, and the earth that is under thee shall be iron. The LORD shall make the rain of thy land powder and dust: from heaven shall it come down upon thee, until thou be destroyed. The LORD shall cause thee to be smitten before thine enemies: thou shalt go out one way against them, and flee seven ways before them: and shalt be removed into all the kingdoms of the earth. And thy carcase shall be meat unto all fowls of the air, and unto the beasts of the earth, and no man shall fray them away. The LORD will smite thee with the botch of Egypt, and with the emerods, and with the scab, and with the itch, whereof thou canst not be healed. The LORD shall smite thee with madness, and blindness, and astonishment of heart: and thou shalt grope at noonday, as the blind gropeth in darkness, and thou shalt not prosper in thy ways: and thou shalt be only oppressed and spoiled evermore, and no man shall save thee. Thou shalt betroth a wife, and another man shall lie with her: thou shalt build an house, and thou shalt not dwell therein: thou shalt plant a vineyard, and shalt not gather the grapes thereof. Thine ox shall be slain before thine eyes, and thou shalt not eat thereof: thine ass shall be violently taken away from before thy face, and shall not be restored to thee: thy sheep shall be given unto thine enemies, and thou shalt have none to rescue them. Thy sons and thy daughters shall be given unto another people, and thine eyes shall look, and fail with longing for them all the day long: and there shall be no might in thine hand. The fruit of thy land, and all thy labours, shall a nation which thou knowest not eat up; and thou shalt be only oppressed and crushed alway: so that thou shalt be mad for the sight of thine eyes which thou shalt see.

Utilize this space to journal and reflect. What are your thoughts after reading this chapter?

_____
_____
_____
_____
_____
_____
_____
_____
_____
_____
_____
_____
_____
_____
_____
_____
_____
_____
_____
_____

CHAPTER 2
The Anatomy of Curses
Dr. Rashia N. Barbee

I did not ask to be born here! I did not ask to be connected to this man and this woman! I did not ask to have this family lineage of curses! I did not ask to be born into this family. I did not ask to be abandoned. I did not ask to be abused. I did not ask to live under this. I inherited this! This is not who I really am. I did not ask to be the black sheep of the family. I would have much rather preferred to be the one who did not have to pay for what happened in the family long before I was born.

It does not matter if it is the first, second, third, or fourth generation, curses continue until someone has the courage to put a stop to them. Generational curses, in most cases, have nothing to do with the generation that the curses fell on. For those who believe in the stories of the Holy Bible, generational curses can be tracked back to the first parents in the bible. Who are the first parents of the bible? Adam and Eve.

You and I were in Adam when he broke God's commandment after listening to Eve. We were condemned with him. Eve yielded to the tempter, the evil serpent, and Adam made a choice to follow her. Prior to being tempted, they were innocent, but temptation provoked them both to make a choice.

Unfortunately, that is how generational curses start and end- by choice. There is not much debate that can be done on that point. Skeletons are in closets now because of a choice. People are tormented by their past because of choices. Some are stuck in cursed environments because of choice.

Choices cause curses.

There are patterns of negative choices that are associated with generational curses. One must identify that something negative is continuing to happen in and around them before they can attempt to break the cycle. There is a root cause to every generational curse, and it starts with a choice. Whether that choice was intended to be a good one, but resulted in a bad one, someone has to learn to live and navigate the consequences of the choice.

Typically, when things are good, everyone wants to take the credit for them. It is very rare that when bad things happen, people are jumping up and down saying, "YES, I DID THAT," with several high fives to one another. In fact, people, in general, have issues with being accountable for their actions, especially when their actions produce curses. The blame game is played in many families today because no one wants to be accountable for what they did or did not do. It is only when one can stop in the midst of a bad continuous cycle and see that something has to change… And the change must start with me.

Negative patterns continue if we choose not to make a change. Just because we were taught certain ways as the right way does not mean it should be executed. Many things we were shown in our childhood were wrong. We did not know it at the time because we were children. We were told to stay in a child's place yet had to embrace error from those who came before us. We carry those same erroneous ways into our adulthood by choice which creates the cycle of curses moving from one generation to the next.

I can remember growing up hearing adults talk about my mother right in front of my younger brother and me. They would say negative things about her parenting, her womanhood, and her personal relationships. Being a child hearing these things come from not just people, but family members was hurtful. I did not know how to process what I was hearing but I began to believe what I was hearing. I even allowed the things I heard to paint a picture of my mother for me. I started to resent my mother at an early age because of it. It was not until I became a young adult that I realized that the narrative being told about my mother was not a whole truth. There were parts left out that she did not get to respond to or even try to vindicate herself in. I began to ask myself the question, if mama was all of these bad things, who taught her? How did she learn this? Where did these habits come from? She, too, was a result of a choice, so why was the choice silenced?

Family history is good to reflect upon as long as only the good is being told. However, if we look across families, not just mine, family history encompasses His-Story, Her-Story, and Their-Story. Family history is made up of everyone's stories. Their versions. Their opinions. Their narratives. When told over and over again, those who are listening for guidance on their journey are being shaped by their history.

In my family, I saw my great-grandmother as a loyal, devoted, and nurturing wife and mother. I thought what she and my great-grandfather had was picture perfect. They had their own house with land; and had established and grown their family. It was not until later in my adult years, I learned that my great-grandfather had a child outside of my great-grandparents' marriage. For all those years of my childhood life, I thought my great-grandparents had the perfect marriage. Well, it was not perfect, but my great grandmother stayed and was faithful to the end.

I often ask myself, being that I most recently went through my own divorce, would I have stayed and remained loyal after learning about betrayal in my marriage? Am I the result of a generational curse because I am divorced? No, I am a result of a choice. So were my mother and my father. **Choices cause curses.**

In the family history, everyone had freewill to make a choice. My maternal great-grandparents stayed together for fifty-plus years until death did they part. My paternal grandparents stayed together for fifty-plus years until death did they part. My parents divorced when I was five years old. I went through a divorce at the age of forty-three. It is all family history, governed by choices.

One thing about choices, if you ever get another chance to make the right choice, you can destroy the cycles of the past. I believe that looking across my lineage, a wholesome marriage belongs to me. My parents might not have experienced it with each other. I may not have experienced it in my first marriage, but my grandparents and great-grandparents have given me hope for a brighter future. I choose to give love a chance again, learn from and not recycle the past.

Let's get back to my mother. I go back here because this is the space I primarily learned from as a child. It governed my adulthood until I decided to unlearn some things. What I learned about the narratives that were shared about my mother is that no one ever gave her credit for the things she chose to do that resulted in good. It was always noted that she borrowed money, borrowed cars, borrowed everything. She was the borrower in the family. She was the one who always needed this or that.

I did not like that narrative. Was my mother a bad person because she was the borrower? Absolutely not! She just did not make the right choices to become the lender. She battled with low self-esteem and really fought in her last years on the earth to reclaim it. And can I just stop right here and salute her?! Mama, you are the reason I chose to do something different and change the narrative for your legacy. Having to be dependent on someone else for finances is the worst ever. I can only imagine how my mother felt trying to mother her two children, provide for them, all while having to continuously ask for help out of the ditch from family members only to be the topic of discussion. I saw and heard too much of it. I decided to find a way where I could destroy that for my family. I was born in it, but I did not have to accept it.

We have accepted what we were born into by loyal default. What is loyal default? It is staying devoted to bad habits because of how the habits were developed and nourished. My mother was loyal to being a borrower by default. I remember my great-grandfather taking my mother to the local town bank to get cash loans for her. I can see us clear as day right now. We all were packed in his red Chevy, windows down, sweating from the summer heat, only for Mama to be able to get through to the next paycheck.

That image would continuously play in my mind every time I experienced financial hardships as an adult. I recognized that my choices were feeding the generational curses that were passed down to me from my mother's choices. I saw it as a child, so I implemented it as an adult, until I had an awakening after my mother's passing in 2018. When people say the death of a parent changes you, especially your mother, believe them. I am not sure if it is because the mother and the child were connected for nine months (or shorter, if the baby was born prematurely). Nevertheless, the connection between a mother and child is deep, so it is with the generational curses passed down to the child.

I was in the middle of pursuing my Masters in Science in Leadership from Pfeiffer University when my mother passed. I told my counselor, Dr. Atkins, I could not finish this without my mother being on the earth to cheer me on. I remember the words he spoke to me then:

"Now how do you think your mother would feel about you quitting if she were here?"

That question hit me in my core. So much so, that from that point on I started implementing ten times the effort on my goals because I had something to prove to myself and my mother's memory. While she never really got the accolades she wanted while here on earth, she left me here to get them for her. This is how I recognized the sign that the generational curses passed down to me can either make me or break me. And this is what we have to decide: is it going to make me into who I am supposed to be or break me all together?

I chose to keep making it for my Mama and was conferred with that Master's degree in July 2019. My mother never went to college, but she was the best Certified Nursing Assistant that I knew. And by the time this book is published, I will have earned my doctorate in Christian Theology. That's for my mama too!

I went through a divorce in 2022 but while going through that divorce, I purchased my first home. My mother never got the opportunity to own her own home. We always rented when I was child. We were even on Section 8. My brother and I always knew when the housing authority lady was coming for inspection because Mama's boyfriend's stuff would be cleared out and the trailer was spotless. Even when I became an adult, my mother always rented a place. So, purchasing my own home was for my Mama too!

I had to find a way to break this financial curse that had been passed down to me. First, I had to enroll into financial classes to learn about credit restoration, budgeting, spending, and managing finances. I started researching jobs that could earn you six figures or more since I had all of my degrees now. What I found is that a JOB meant Just Over Broke, so I had to change my focus if I was determined to break this financial generational curse. My mama always worked jobs, sometimes three at a time, but she was always still the "borrower." After closing on my house in 2022, I began to seek the Lord in prayer and fasting about my financial trajectory. I had accomplished a major milestone in my life, and I was not about to be in a place of worrying over how I was going to pay my mortgage. After all, it was not just me; it was also my boys. I worked hard to purchase my home. I was determined to keep it and own multiple homes. We are talking about breaking generational curses here, right? Okay, keep reading.

The Lord brought back to my remembrance an opportunity that was presented to me over six years ago by way of the life insurance industry. Six years ago was not my time but in 2022, God said, "It's your time to shine in this entrepreneurial space for real this time."

I write "this time" because I tried my hand at entrepreneurship a few years back, failed and went back to Corporate America to work a job. Now let me be clear here, if working a job is what you want to do and it is working for you, stay there. However, for the remnant that is saying, I am working this job or these jobs in some cases, but I am still struggling financially, take note of what has been passed down to you and adjust accordingly.

In 2022, I became a licensed life insurance agent in the states of North Carolina, South Carolina, Georgia, Virginia, Maryland, and New Jersey. It was the ticket that allowed a person to write their own paycheck, as big or small as you want it. Since being licensed and working my business full time since April 2022, I have set myself up to be financially stable. I have not had to ask anyone to pay my mortgage, utility bills, car note, or to buy groceries, and even have money set aside for emergencies. I chose to do it differently to get different. Seeing my mother struggle as the black sheep for years of my life propelled me to go hard after something different.

Here's a nugget for you, if what you went through does not propel you to be better, then going through it was a waste! Going through should take on a whole new meaning when you really want to get through and break the cycle. We can say as many times as we want, that we are tired of our lives being this way. However, it is only when we decide to make a change that things will change.

Remember...**Choices cause curses.**

There comes a time when the choice to not be under the curse has to show up. You are the choice. I am the choice. It is time for us to destroy, demolish, throw out and up anything that keeps us cursed and not blessed. I know it may be a little challenging at first to see yourself on the other side of the curse but take the blinders of the past off. See your future as bright as the sun shines every day. Go after it! Do not settle for what was passed to you. Do not even hold your hand out. Hold your hand up to catch the plan God has for you and your life and run it. It is a good plan, a plan of hope and not of evil. You are not the curse; you are the choice. Choose to be the chain breaker!

Generational curses have formed our lives, but it is now our time to reform our lives without them. We have learned that none of the curses passed down to us were our fault. It is up to us to own how the curses of past generations will not repeat with us. As long as we are still breathing, we have another chance to break what has been built from the past. In fact, we should be on a mission to not just break the generational curses cycle but destroy them.

I started this writing by making "I did not" statements because the reality is none of us asked for any generational curses that were passed down to us. We did not want to have curses associated with us but by nature and choice, that has happened. So where does it start? How do we end it? Can we end it? I believe we can because we all have a choice.

I choose to break this off me. I choose to not pass this down to my children so they will not pass it down to their children. I choose to work on my traumas from the past and the present to go into a curse-free future. I choose to unlearn the bad methodologies and ideologies of my forefathers. They worked for them then, but they do not work for me now. I choose to reform my lineage with powerful affirmations of who I AM and not where I came from. I choose to put in the work to break the negative patterns of my past. I make the same choice to end the continuous battle of defeat over my life that started the curse. It is all about the choice and what follows.

I am the starting point of something new. I am getting out this time for good. The curse stops with me because I choose for it to. Yes, I was born here. Yes, this is my family. Yes, there are traumas of the past that have followed me. Yes, someone else's disobedience caused some bad things to attach themselves to me. However, I have a choice in the matter. I choose to break it with no intention of fixing it so that it cycles me back to a broken state of mind, spirit, and soul. It was structured for me to stay in the cycle of the curse, but I choose to deconstruct, remove, and rebuild a new person for the generations that come after me to follow.

Arise future generations, we have chosen to make it better for you!

Utilize this space to journal and reflect. What are your thoughts after reading this chapter?

CHAPTER 3
Healing Through Awareness
ShaQuandra Dawson

For most people, family is the most important thing in life. We deeply cherish the family unit that we know and grew up in. We carry the values and attitudes with us that were instilled into us in childhood for our entire lives. The way we think, act, and see the world has origins in what we were taught as children.

Unfortunately, some of what is taught to us may not be what's best for us despite our caretaker's best efforts. For many of us, we've been conditioned into living and thinking in ways that are actually damaging to our growth as individuals. Our lives are a culmination of all of the things we saw and were taught as we grew up. Generational curses passed down, sometimes through decades, have a negative effect on our lives and tend to stunt our growth, preventing us from reaching our full potential as adults.

Generational curses and trauma can be passed down knowingly or unknowingly by those who raised us. Many of them become set in how they were raised without giving deeper thought to the negative impacts that certain behaviors had on them. They then place those same negative expectations on their children.

In the study of population, health researchers look at the outcomes of people groups based on a variety of health determinants. These include things such as environment, childhood, socioeconomic status, and education, to name a few. This highlights the fact that the health outcomes of individuals are not solely based on the choices they made but factors out of their control as well.

We can also apply this logic when we look at the outcomes of our lives outside of the concept of health. The adults we grow into and the lives we live are related to the choices we made, but also the families we grew up in. Family dynamics and values have heavily influenced those choices. Ideally, that influence would be a positive one, giving us proper guidance to ultimately live happy, fulfilled lives with healthy, meaningful relationships. Unfortunately, sometimes we come from families with negative generational cycles that cause stress and turmoil for us as we navigate through life.

The challenge comes when we no longer wish to operate in these destructive patterns and decide that we want to break the mold and live our lives differently. Though it can be tough, it is possible.

One of the first and most important steps in making the change is taking a closer look at ourselves through self-evaluation. Self-evaluation is the process of analyzing our feelings, thoughts, and behaviors and reflecting on how they affect our day-to-day lives. While your amount of success can be considered, the self-evaluation should be a holistic look into oneself rather than focusing on surface level things such as status or achievements.

Through this process, you may think about personality traits. Are you assertive or passive? Are you emotionally intelligent? Do you have trouble developing lasting healthy relationships, whether they be romantic or platonic? Do you struggle with setting boundaries? Do you struggle with addiction? Are you able to control your anger?

You may also consider your financial situation: do you struggle with making and managing money? Do you live paycheck to paycheck? Are you able to keep a steady job?

Being honest about the answers to these questions leads us to become self-aware.

Self-awareness is defined as conscious knowledge of one's own character, feelings, motives, and desires. Reaching self-awareness is the first stage in breaking negative generational cycles. We must be aware of our own destructive actions and patterns in order to evolve and break the generational cycles that led us to developing these patterns.

There will be a time when you will have an "ah-ha" moment. ethics you came up in a family that suffered with poverty and then one day it hits you that this has been due to poor work ethic, lack of accountability, and poor money management skills. Maybe barely anyone in your family can maintain healthy long-lasting relationships despite wanting them. Then you realize this is due to a lack of emotional intelligence while consistently making poor choices in partners. Maybe your family has been separated into "cliques" for many years versus being a cohesive unit and being selectively supportive. Whatever the struggle may be, whether big or small, we must look at these patterns in our personal lives and assess our families.

What you see as destructive behavior and generational curses may not be as apparent to everyone else in your family. It is very likely that most of your family who have lived in dysfunction for their entire lives will make excuses such as, "Well, that's just the way we are." This may require separation between you and certain family members while you are on your journey to becoming self-aware. I recently heard a sermon by Sarah Jakes Roberts, and she said something that stood out to me:

"Starve out the people who feed things that make you unstable."

When God has put you on the mission of becoming your family's generational curse breaker and you are on the road to learning yourself, tracking your patterns and behaviors, and becoming aware of what creates negative emotions inside of you, you'll have to starve the people out of your life who feed negative patterns and behaviors, who trigger you and enable the negative behaviors of others. Just love those family members from a distance and press on. Unfortunately, not everyone can see your vision and the need for change.

An example from my own life where I am breaking a generational cycle is choosing not to physically hit my children as a form of punishment. This tends to be difficult for many of my family members to grasp. As a child, I grew up in a household where physical punishment was used. If I did wrong, I got a "whoopin" which is the norm in the black community. It is thought that this form of punishment raises respectful children, when really it just instills fear and insecurity in them.

Unfortunately, this was part of the reason I remained silent while going through years of sexual abuse as a child. My abuser said that if I told anyone what occurred, I'd be in trouble. At seven-years-old, I understood that meant my mom would whoop me and the thought of that was enough to keep me quiet for a long time. I didn't have the ability to discern whether what he was saying was true or not.

While physical punishment was not the cause of the abuse that I suffered, it did make me an easier target to be abused due to the fear that I had of being punished. This traumatic experience shaped the way that I see the world as an adult. There are very few people that I trust, especially with my children. Though I try not to push my trauma onto them, sometimes it can be hard because I am so determined to make sure that they never have to go through sexual abuse, or any kind of abuse, as I did. Thankfully through lots of prayer, therapy, and my resilient spirit, I have been able to move past this experience and create a decent life for myself with my mental health still mostly intact.

Now as an adult, I choose to use gentle/respectful parenting with my own children. This does not mean that I allow them to run wild and that there are no consequences for their actions. It means I give them grace and foster a safe, respectful environment for them to live and grow in. I have chosen to make myself knowledgeable about what is developmentally appropriate in children, something generations before me did not or could not do.

For example, my nine-year-old will haphazardly clean his room because he wants to go outside. When I see that the room is still not clean, but he is gone outside, do I beat him? No, I make him come back inside and do it correctly. There are also times when my two-year-old has a tantrum, as toddlers tend to do. I don't beat her. I let her have the tantrum. Then once she calms down, I tell her why she can't have chocolate at seven o'clock in the morning and offer her an alternative.

Of course, just grabbing a belt and beating them would be a lot easier, requiring much less patience and talking, but in the long run, it's inefficient for two reasons. On one hand, it instills fear. A child who fears you will hide things from you. On the other hand, we must be aware that our children will one day grow into adults. This is what many parents tend to forget. Our children will not be children forever. If we want to raise healthy, strong-willed, successful adults, we cannot beat them into submission in childhood and expect them to thrive and advocate for themselves in the adult world.

Being the first in my immediate family to choose to parent this way definitely comes with some side eyes from my family, but the situation has improved over time with education. As for distant family, anyone who feels negatively about my choice to not hit my child, just like Sarah Jakes Roberts said, I starve them out of my and my children's lives. You must know what your mission is, what you're trying to change, and why; and don't allow any negativity from the outside to change your mind, especially when you know that you're making the right decision to facilitate change for you and your family.

Once you reach the point of self-awareness, you can then move on to actually breaking the generational curse as I'm doing with gentle parenting.

So now that you are aware that these cycles exist, you must start to make changes with yourself first. As stated above, everyone will not see the need for change or even see a problem, so start with yourself.

If you are trying to break a generational curse of an endless cycle of poverty, you may start by changing your work ethic, pursuing higher education, or learning about financial literacy, such as budgeting, saving, and making smart investments rather than spending frivolously.

If you are trying to break a generational curse of sexual abuse, you may start by keeping your children away from and advising other family members to keep their kids away from the "creepy uncle" that all of the older females in the family have a story about. You may also stop allowing your kids to participate in sleep overs and teaching them body awareness; as well as what's appropriate and what's not to protect them against predators (which for some reason has been frowned upon within the black community for some reason). In order to break destructive cycles, we must trade most, if not all, of the negative behaviors that we have become accustomed to with positive ones that promote change and healing.

During this process of healing, you must understand that the transition from becoming self-aware to breaking generational curses may not be a seamless one. There may be times where you consciously make a decision that may not be the best. As the saying goes, old habits are hard to break. I find this to be especially true when trying to break certain emotional behaviors.

If you were raised in a chaotic, violent home and naturally grew into a chaotic violent adult, it may be difficult to keep calm when provoked. Similarly, if you were raised in a very unloving, unaffectionate home with no one to trust, it may be difficult for you as an adult to build relationships without building a wall and blocking out those who are trying to love you.

During these times, you must give yourself grace. These habits have been formed over time–over the course of years, sometimes decades based on how you were raised and taught as a child. The process of breaking these generational curses will certainly not happen overnight. This process will be difficult. But the important part is to actually make strides to improve your thoughts, feelings, and behaviors in order to become a better you. And it starts with the first step, becoming self-aware.

Therapy is a very important piece to breaking generational curses. Once you have that awareness regarding all of the dysfunction that has gone on around you for decades, it may cause a lot of mental and emotional upset for you. Speaking with a licensed therapist can help you sort through all of those emotions and unpack them. This will also help teach you how to deal with these emotions and potentially how to deal with the family members who have been the source of the dysfunction.

Now that you have become self-aware and have begun working on breaking the generational curses in your life, this will likely give you the courage to speak up to dysfunctional family members and hopefully lead many of them to a place of healing for themselves. This is one of the positive outcomes of becoming aware of yourself. Sure, everyone will not be receptive to change but there will be those who too have wanted to live differently and have a different outcome for the family. Maybe they themselves struggled with self-evaluation and awareness. With you being the person who has reached the level of self-awareness to heal and break the generational curses, you can help lead them to that same healing.

Utilize this space to journal and reflect. What are your thoughts after reading this chapter?

_____

_____

_____

_____

_____

_____

_____

_____

_____

_____

_____

_____

_____

_____

_____

_____

_____

_____

_____

CHAPTER 4
Rewriting Family Narratives
Travis Wofford

What happens in this house stays in this house...

"You never want other people all in your business" is what they would say. So, if Uncle Man Man was using drugs, you didn't want anyone outside of the house to know it. Someone could have lost their job and could use a hand. But we can't say anything to anyone because you don't want them talking about you.

Blood is thicker than water...

Blood is thicker than water is one of the oldest phrases around and GOD only knows how many times it has been used by people to make a point. We've all heard this phrase plenty of times! That's your family, you always have to look out for your family no matter what. That doesn't always hold true because sometimes your blood will be the first one to try and take advantage of you and get over you. Ask yourself these questions. If someone in your family wrongs you, are you supposed to just take it and accept it because you're blood related? Especially if they refuse to accept responsibility for their actions. Does that mean family can do certain things and you're supposed to forgive because it's family? Blood is thicker than water but sometimes your true family is not your blood.

Never ask about nor discuss your money with family...

What makes money so taboo that you can't discuss it with the people you interact with the most, your family? Some people are living, and some are surviving. I feel that this is a survival mindset, this is survival mode. If you want something different you have to do something different. I feel that money definitely should be discussed, and it should be discussed often. Financial literacy is something that needs to be discussed and taught but if the ones who should be teaching don't know any better than how they will teach. So, to just make it easier they say don't discuss it. "You don't want to make people feel uncomfortable." Sometimes people feel uncomfortable discussing money and finance because of the lack of it. They're just trying to make it to next week without something going wrong.

These are all things I'm sure many of us have heard growing up. As a child, I know I heard all of these sayings and more. In our adolescent and even young adult years, these are some of the things that we are taught. When the people who are teaching you and molding you don't know any better, the cycle of bad family narratives continues until someone is able to rewrite them. With all these sayings comes some truth, but there are always exceptions. You don't want the entire world in your personal business or knowing your every move in general. Some people mean you are no good, even some people in your family. You have to find the right people to discuss things with. Your family should come first, the ones that come with good intent and really want to see you excel in life, but once again you have to find the right one. Some people want to see you doing good, just not better than them. Money should always be discussed with everyone and watch who you take advice from. Once again you have to find the right people to have those conversations with.

Our family is supposed to be the base of each of us in our young years. I'm speaking of adolescence more because that's when we start to get our shape. When I say shape, I don't mean physically, but our mind. The things we're taught and what we take in. Family is supposed to be there to help you learn right from wrong. Help mold you into a productive person and teach you to think for yourself. Give you the tools you need to be able to go out into the world and make a difference when you grow up.

For the most part, this is true in most families but what happens when your family doesn't know how to do these things for themselves? What happens if none of them are equipped with the tools that it takes to make a positive impact on the world? How will they teach someone else something they have never been taught?

There's always an exception to the rule! There's always that one who thinks stuff differently. Who feels like they are different from the people around them. At first, they really can't put their finger on it, but it burns just a little bit down inside of them. And it's not that they feel like they're better, just different. They look at things differently, then about everyone else, they notice things most don't see. They say something about it at first but normally people may tell them they're crazy. They may ask, why do you say that? Or, why do you think like that? This, more than likely, will make them stop speaking up, not wanting to draw attention to themselves.

As years go on, the burning gets stronger and it begins to make them feel as if they are crazy, as if something is wrong. They start to ask themselves the same questions, why do I see things like that? They even try to put out the fire that's in them, but the one thing about the fire they didn't account for is that they didn't put it in themselves. It was put there by God, so they can never put it out. They can fight it, but nothing they do will put it out! It takes finding someone who really knows what's going on to help them because everyone else has no clue! Once they meet that person who can help articulate what's going on, that's when they realize they have been put on this earth to not be regular! To not fit in with everyone else, to not fit inside someone's box. Once they realize all that, then they start to understand they are Curse Breakers!

I would love to tell you once you realize you're a curse breaker, everything falls right into place and gets easier; unfortunately, it doesn't happen that way. What we fail to realize is that over the years, we've been programmed to replicate the same behavior and adopt the same mannerism that we see in others around us. Most of the time, the people we find ourselves duplicating are our family. The good, the bad and the ugly. Now I'm not saying that being like people in our families is bad, most of them have good ways and intentions but some mindsets are not always good. Some of the traditions are not always good. Take, for example, the way some people eat. Back in the day, some people didn't have a lot of options on what they put inside the body but even as they got more options, some still stuck with the traditions of the food they grew up on no matter what effect it had on their body. I can't sit on a high horse and say I'm not guilty of it myself, it's just when we know better, we have to do better. We see the effects it has on the people we love, and we still choose to consume it on a daily basis. It takes someone to show a different way of getting true nourishment into our body, so we don't have to go through the same ordeals the past generations went through.

Such as high blood pressure, hypertension, diabetes and obesity which can lead to a rough life and sometimes death. If we want to live a long and prosperous life, we have to be aware of what we are putting in our bodies. We need to learn better eating habits that can be fuel to our bodies and not poison.

It's not just about what we eat that can poison us, the things we whisper about but turn a blind eye to. I mean dark traditions or things we've been conditioned to, for example. Cousin Betty always has a black eye, but no one says anything about it because what goes on between a husband and wife is no one's business. Even worse, telling Cousin Betty that divorce is a sin so she can't leave her husband because they believe God's word won't allow it. If they wanted to really follow the word, they know GOD wants us to 'honor thy wife.' If someone truly loves you, they will never intentionally hurt you. That's a lesson that needs to be passed down generation to generation.

Some of this can even spill over into the next generation. You try to bring a girl/guy home, and everyone is telling you that you guys can't date but no one tells you why. Then when you get older, you hear whispers that you guys are illegitimate cousins, but no one talks about it. They don't tell you how Ms. Losie used to live next door and grandpa would get caught sneaking out of the house at night. Then she pops up pregnant and the baby has a striking resemblance to his other children. To keep his wife from seeing it every day, Ms. Losie takes the baby and moves across town. Everyone hears the whispers, but no one says anything until the next generation comes along. Now they see each other at school, not knowing they are related, and no one has the heart to tell them the truth. They just say, stay away from them., This makes kids want to be with each other more. When all someone had to do was tell them the truth.

Traditions like following the preacher blindly, never questioning what he says or does. Even though they say he has another family on the other side of town.

These are examples of trauma or triggers that we all experience in some shape, form or fashion when you're growing up. Then once you want to do things differently from everyone around you, some may say, you're moving or acting funny. Some may say that you think you're better than others. Just because you want better for yourself doesn't mean you think you're better.

Then once you get a little older, you can start to make most of your own decisions. I say 'most' because you still don't want to buck against the system too much, especially if you still live at home. By your teen years, you start to look at things differently. You begin to question why this or why that. You wonder why the world is the way it is and if you live in a certain environment, why are you living the way you are? You also may find yourself mimicking a lot of what you see your family doing. Because if you still don't know who you truly are yet and what your purpose is, it's easy to be led by what you see others doing. For example, if most of your family smokes cigarettes, more than likely you will try them as well. Same goes for alcohol: if most of the people in your family drink, you will likely drink too. We mimic what we see, good, bad or ugly we can pick up those traits. We can also break them but if you really want a different life for yourself, you can do it.

It takes a minute, but your eyes start to notice things. Such as Uncle Tim is on oxygen because he's been a cigarette smoker since he was ten. Aunt Pat has cirrhosis of the liver due to heavy drinking. We all see these things, yet some of us still choose to follow that path.

One of the biggest things you can get from your family and the people around you is a mindset. There's a saying that goes, "It's not what happens to you in life that breaks or makes you, it's how you react to it when it happens." All of this has to do with mindset. Do you have a positive mindset? Do you say, "I'm going to get through this! It will not break me!"? Or do you have the mind of, "I'm not going to make it through this. This is going to break me."? One thing that's certain, the older you get, life is going to happen.

Sometimes the people in your life can have what I call the victim mindset. They feel like life is always picking on them, beating them down and they don't have too much in life to look forward to. Our mind is the most powerful thing we have from which comes the words we speak into the world. A lot of people struggle with this especially in low-income environments. They can get caught up in the struggles of trying to make ends meet and more than likely are living check to check. Most of the time, they just have enough to pay their bills and put food on the table. Anything other than that is a struggle. So, when (not if) something happens out of the usual, they're unprepared. It could be anything that can completely throw everything off for the week or for the entire month. It can take a minute to recover from or even have to borrow from Peter to pay Paul.

For example, the car breaks down and this is their only form of transportation. If it breaks down on the side of the road, it has to be towed, which is an unexpected expense. Once it gets to the shop, the cost of the repair can really put a strain on them. On top of that, they have to find a way to get to work and wherever else they need to go. All of this can have someone thinking, "Why me? I have the worst luck. Nothing good ever happens to me. How am I going to get through this?" A flip to that is, if you think about it more positively, "It could have broken down and caused me to have an accident. At least I still have my job, I'll figure out how I'm going to get to work. I'm not going to stress about it because my needs are met. Life is always life-ing!" How your mind handles a situation can make it better or worse. I'm not saying it's easy to be optimistic but it's better than being pessimistic. Look up at the sky. When you're looking up you can see things differently. There's more to see—birds, eagles, planes. All these things are moving, going somewhere. This means you have your head held high compared to looking at the ground. When you have your head down in defeat, you only see the ground and what lives down there. Worms, snakes, small insects, nothing optimistic (unless you find some money). Other than that, I don't see the benefit. Regardless of what you go through, face it head up, chest out! You will make it to the other side, I promise.

Stress and worry are traits that can definitely be passed down. If we see our parents always stressing and worrying, we as children will likely be the same. However, if the parents have a positive outlook on life and are speaking life into situations, the children will more than likely do the same. It's not always what you go through in life, sometimes it's how you handle what you go through. Life will have its stressful moments but learning how to handle those moments will make them a lot less stressful. You also have to learn to appreciate the good moments. When things are going your way, it is important to take time to live in those moments. Don't use that time worrying about what bad thing will happen next.

Your mindset is a choice: you can choose light over darkness. The light is already inside of us. We have to be willing to let it shine even in those dark moments. When everything around you is going wrong, we still have to remember that the light that shines inside is there to get us through. Even in darkness you can let your light shine and it will help guide you through. Even if everyone is speaking negatively around you or even speaking it to you, we have to find that glimmer of light to get you through. God sends us light, we just have to be conscious to recognize it and understand it comes in the forms of people, events and opportunities.

At this stage in our lives, we are interested in the opposite sex. Guys look at girls differently than when they were adolescents and vice versa. I'm sure we all had our crushes when we were younger but when you get to a certain age, you are ready to act on these urges. Once again we go by what we were taught. I can't say how it is for women, but when I was coming up, no man really taught me how to treat a woman, how to provide, protect, respect and honor them to the highest. I was told, "You better get all you can get while you can get it." That was the motto I and a lot of young men lived by for most of our teenage and young adult years. Playing the field and having fun. Women do this as well but I'm not sure what their talk was like coming up. And truly, they play the field better than most men. Most women are more organized than most men. So, when it comes to playing the field, they have an advantage. Most men are pretty simple to figure out: we like what we like, and we all have patterns. Most of the time, women study us and learn our behaviors, our patterns. So, when we start to move differently they pick up on it pretty quickly. They may not know what's different, but they know something is. They can also be more cunning; they plan their moves while we, as men, mostly act on impulse and figure the rest out later. Most of the time, that's how men get caught. I'm not saying women don't get caught but often, it's the men who are caught up. Once again it's what we see and are used to.

I don't remember seeing a lot of happy couples growing up. I saw a lot of married couples, but they didn't seem to be happily married. This can lead to someone stepping out of the marriage, which can lead to trauma. A majority of the time, this can come from us all not having the skills to communicate in a marriage. As men, we're told to suck it up and get over it. Women may hear, "Don't step out of a woman's place and stand by your husband." Once the new generation sees all of that going on, they feel as if they don't want to go through any of it, so they hurt before they get hurt. Which perpetuates the cycle of "Hurt People Hurting People," until we get to a certain point in life where we want to settle down or we think we found that Mr. or Mrs. Right. That's when we start to look at things in a different light. Then again some never get to that point and decide to continue the cycle.

One thing we never truly talked about was finances, and we definitely never truly heard about entrepreneurship. Most people have a job but that was it, just a job. Clock in, do your time, clock out and go home, then do it all over again the next day. Never trying to live their purpose, really just trying to survive until they get paid again. Sometimes it's hard for people to have the confidence to step out on faith to start their own business. To truly bet on themselves and take that leap to have control of their own lives. To remove the top from the jar and spread their wings. To live life to their highest potential and call their own shoots!! It can be scary and it's not always pretty. You just have to find that all the sacrifices will be worth it.

Growing up, we didn't talk about how much money someone had. It was considered rude. In some respects, it may still be that way, depending on who you ask, but this generation is more into sharing financial literacy with others. Most people are thought to always be in survival mode. Save as much money as you can in the bank for a rainy day but rarely talk about starting a business or investing in one. Don't get me wrong, there will always be self-innovated people with the will to make things happen by any means necessary, but they're called hustlers. You know, bootlegger, moonshine maker, poker houses–all entrepreneurs but on the wrong side of the law. That carries over to our generation that really didn't want to do what others told them to do. Didn't want to move or jump when they were told to do so. They found ways of making money on their own. Some good, some bad but we're still going off what we were programmed to do. We need to start normalizing families getting together and talking about getting a trust started. We need to educate ourselves in the stock market and learn what to invest in. Grow our real estate portfolio and hold on to it instead of selling the first chance we get. Start being able to leave the generation coming up with the tools, the teachings and skills to make it to the next level in life. The generation behind them can then have the opportunity to go higher than they did. Even if one generation loses it all, they will be prepared to get it back and then some.

Another tool we need in our arsenal to make it through this thing called life that we may not have seen is a sense of gratitude! We have to learn this because if you haven't been taught this, it will make it hard to navigate through life. You have to recognize when God puts people, opportunities and events in our path to help us. We have to learn to be thankful for what we have and who we have in our lives. If all your needs are met we have to be thankful and rejoice for that. Give GOD the praise for all he has done and currently doing in your life. This will also help you look at things through another lens. If all we do is talk about what you don't have then you fail to miss out on the blessing you do have. Give him praise and glory and watch the blessing keep coming but you still have to do your part as well.

For example, you may not get people in your family to speak life into you but the lady up the street is always speaking life into you. You may not have a car to get around in, but your next-door neighbor lets you ride with them to work. You may not have the job you want but your supervisor lets you stay over and learn how to operate the new machine to add value to you in the company. We have to recognize these things and give thanks in order to continue to receive them.

Think about it for a second: if someone invites you over and cooks you a three-course meal from scratch including dessert, sets the table and serves it to you, but you get up from the table and walk out without a word, I'm pretty sure that's the last time they will invite you over. You didn't say it was good, offer thanks for the meal, or nothing. Just got up and left without showing any type of gratitude.

Now let's flip it, they invite you over, cook the same three-course meal with dessert, set the table and serve you. Once it's over, you rave how good the food was and you even ask to take some home with you. You tell them thank you and let them know you appreciate all the time and effort they put into it. I can pretty much guarantee that they will invite you back over for dinner. They will more than likely try to outdo the first meal they made. All of that because of a simple gesture of gratitude. We can't put a price on it if we tried, but, at the same time, it does not cost a dime. We all need to practice this, but we all may not have been taught this in our lives. We have to break the cycle of not showing gratitude or thanks.

A majority of us who were raised in certain economic struggles were told to bring all our extra money into the storehouse to save for a rainy day. Make sure you have enough for you and yours, don't worry about no one else! They are not your problem or your responsibility. If you give yours away, then you won't have anything for yourself when it rains. Most people whose families didn't have a lot; this was their way of thinking. "People need to learn to take care of themselves," they would say, which I'm not disagreeing with. If you're an adult, you should be able to take care of yourself. Unfortunately, life happens to all of us, and sometimes no matter how much you plan, it will get you down at some point. So, if you see someone down, do you help? Do you give from what you have, or do you walk by like you don't see them? Or even worse, you give it to them while posting their picture on social media to let everyone know you did it. We don't always know people's stories and how they got to the palace they're at but what we do know is we're all children of the Most High and should try to be of service to one another if we can.

I was told later in life, if you want more, you need to give more! At the time, it made no sense to me at all. I was struggling and just trying to make it so how could I give more to take me to the next level? As I got older and got more things in life, I realized that being able to be a blessing to others gave me something that I never expected. It gave me a sense of appreciation for everything I have! I not only enjoy giving to people who are in need, but I enjoy giving to people who just need someone to do something nice for them. It's not always money that's a blessing but the kind gesture that is behind it!

To be able to pay for a complete stranger's meal and see their face light up is a blessing to me! For years, I tried to hold on to and squeeze as much as I could out of every dollar I had because that's what I was taught. But as I got older, what I realized was that while I had my hands clenched trying to hold onto that $1, if I opened my hands God would place $100 in it! Don't get me wrong, I'm not saying give all your money away, that doesn't make sense at all. But if you can do something nice for someone, be a blessing to someone, be that glimmer of light in a dark time, you may realize you get a lot more back than you give out!

These are some of the things I see as I walk through this thing called life. I have realized I wasn't put here to be average. I wasn't put here to be like everyone else before me but to break generational curses, and to change the narrative for my kids and my kids' kids!

> *Our deepest fear is not that we are inadequate. Our deepest fear is that we are powerful beyond measure. It's our light not our darkness that most frightens us!*
> *-Marianne Williamson*

Utilize this space to journal and reflect. What are your thoughts after reading this chapter?

CHAPTER 5
The Path to Forgiveness
Dawanna Alexander

The definition of forgiveness is the action or process of forgiving or being forgiven.

When you think about forgiveness, what's the first thing that comes to mind? I know for most of you, you might be saying, "I can't forgive them for what they have done to me because they hurt me and guess what we all have been hurt to the point of what we thought was no return. I'm sure you're thinking, "Yeah, right, I'm not forgiving NOBODY," because that's the exact same thing I used to say: "I WILL NEVER FORGIVE THEM FOR WHAT THEY DID TO ME.

For me, I truly had a hard time with the word forgiveness, but after having a conversation with a friend one day, it hit me like a ton of bricks: ``What if God didn't forgive me?" We have a father who forgives us time and time again and yet we still let him down. Once we learn to get rid of the flesh and allow God to come in, that's when things will change. We always forget to ask that his will be done, not ours. That's what keeps us from forgiving because we try to do things our way and not God's way. And that itself can cause us more pain we don't even have to go through. Then we get mad at God because we feel as if he doesn't love or care for us, but God loves us even when we don't deserve to be loved.

Matthew 6:14-15 states 'for if ye forgive men their trespasses, your heavenly Father will also forgive you. but if ye forgive not men their trespasses, neither will your Father forgive your trespasses.' When we don't forgive others, we allow them to have power over us, we allow them to keep us in a dark place. You see, what we don't often understand is that forgiveness is needed in order to move on. Not forgiving is first and foremost unhealthy. Forgiving is for you, not them. When we learn to forgive and let God handle the rest, everything else will fall into place. When we don't forgive, and we keep holding onto it, this causes us to carry other people's burdens. Galatians 6:5 says,

> *For every man shall bear his own burden. Galatians 6:5*
>
> *Take heed to yourselves: If thy bother trespass against thee, rebuke him; and if he repent, forgive him. And if he trespass against thee seven times in a day turn again to thee, saying I repent thou shalt forgive him. Luke 17:3-4*

Not only did I have to learn to forgive, but I also had to learn how to unburden the weight of my past. No, it was not easy, and truth be told there are still days that can be hard but that's when I lean and depend on God. My past has taught me so much: at an early age, I was a mother of two wonderful kids, married to a man who I thought loved me, only to find out he cared nothing about me or my children. One year after coming back from the beach for our anniversary, he sat me down and said, "What if I told you I have a baby on the way?"

I knew that I wasn't pregnant, so I asked, "What do you mean you have a baby on the way?"

Mind you, he had been cheating on me the entire time with different ladies that he worked with. Some even said he was sleeping with the man next door. I didn't understand why I thought we were happy. I was a great wife, I worked, cleaned the house, made sure my family had hot meals every day.

I also did not know at the time that he was on drugs. I had a friend who would always say that she went to the store with this dude and that he did a line in front of her, but she would never come out and say, "Girl, your husband is on drugs." Maybe she didn't know how to tell me, but months went by, and she started asking me if he ate when I cooked and if his feet were cold. I didn't really know how to take all this, but she just said, "Pay attention."

Needless to say, I began paying close attention. That's when I realized there were days that I cleaned up and would find his plate tucked away in the dresser drawer. One day, I questioned him about the food and that's when he told me that he was doing drugs, and it was my fault.

My heart was broken; I felt like it had been ripped out. Here I was with two kids and a failed marriage. I began to question God and ask him, "Why me?" Then I was reminded, "Why not you?". In that moment, I had to learn that people can only treat you how you allow them to treat you. That's when I learned my worth and I promised myself that I would never depend on a man to take care of me and my kids. I made sure I would work to take care of us. Things were hard: I did everything in my power to take care of us.

Then I was diagnosed with Graves' Disease. It almost killed me... BUT GOD! There were days that I couldn't do anything. I would lay on the bathroom floor throwing up and my baby girl was right by my side. I had to depend on my mom to cook and help get the kids a bath and get them ready for school the next day. Once again, I had to learn how to pick up the pieces.

When I was first diagnosed with Graves' Disease, I really didn't know what it was. All the doctor told me was that l had to have radiation treatment by the end of that week. That's how bad it was. He looked me and my mom in the face and said, "Sounds like Graves' Disease, looks like Graves' Disease. Yeah, you have Graves' Disease."

I asked him if had anything we could read up on and he said, "No, all you need to know is that it's common for your age range."

I didn't know what that meant; all I could do was put all the blame on my ex-husband. I thought that he was the reason I was sick. At the time, when I researched everything, all that came up was about stress, so could it be that I had done it to myself?

But really who in their right mind would want to make themselves sick? Now that would be a hard pill to swallow because he was off living his best life, while I was sick and struggling to take care of my kids. As I began to research what I was dealing with, I realized that I worried and stressed so much about everything that I did it to myself. That's when I truly began to understand what forgiveness really was. It was hard but I knew that I had to forgive my ex-husband and everyone who had ever hurt me.

So, I picked up the broken pieces of my life and began to heal. I allowed God to lead me, and it felt good to be in that place with God. I started going back to church every Sunday. Forgiveness starts with you. I know that it's not easy to forgive and it seems like people bounce back fast, but it's a process and trust me, it doesn't happen overnight.
To fully forgive, a lot of times people need to be delivered from the things that have broken them. When I gave my life to Christ, I was delivered and once I let all that stuff go, it was like a weight had been lifted off of me. I felt so good, I was back to myself. I was in a very good place in my life, and I was finally able to move on from my past.

I told myself that I was good, that I didn't need or want a man to define who I was but being in the church and looking for God to help me through, that's when the enemy sends you someone to take you off course. I failed the test—I allowed a young man to come into our lives.

He said everything you could imagine, all the things a woman would dream of her man saying. It was a dream come true to have a man willing to cook clean and help take care of your kids. But as we know that all good things come to an end, an end I never imagined in a million years came.

I got a call one morning from my son who was at school, saying that he needed to tell me something. He said, "I wanted to tell you last night, but I waited until today because I knew you would be at work and that it would upset you." He wanted to make sure that I would be alright.

Not knowing what he was about to say I told him that no matter what he was about to tell me, I would be alright. My heart was beating so fast, I really didn't know what to expect. I took a deep breath, and he said, "I was going through my sister's phone last night and I was reading her text message and I think she has been raped."

My heart stopped at the words that a mother never wants to hear.

My son said, "I know you're upset but don't worry cause I'm going to kill him when I see him."

At that moment, I became angry and bitter, and I forgot the meaning of forgiveness, because I wanted to blow his head off. I was so sick to my stomach; I didn't know what to say or do.

My manager at the time was truly amazing and I thank God for her that day. She took me and her arms, prayed and covered me. She locked me in her office and told me that I was not able to leave her office until I got myself together and promised her I would not go to his job and kill him. She said, "Now is not the time for you to kill him. If you kill or hurt him, what's going to happen with your kids? Now is your time to be there and help them get through this."

I didn't know where to begin so I started by going to check my baby girl out from school to ask her if anybody ever touched her or done things to her that they were not supposed to do. She said, "Yes."

Again, my heart stopped. I knew at this point, I needed to protect her, so I called my mom and my sister and told them what I had just found out

That night, my sister came to our house, and we talked about what was going to happen over the next few days. The next day, I took my daughter to the police department so we could file a report because there was no way I was going to allow him to get off Scot-free with what he had done to my baby. The detective was so amazing, she asked me what made me believe what I was told. She said, "You will not believe the amount of people who come in here and don't believe what their kids say."

I told her that I believed it because my daughter didn't tell it, my son did and even if she did tell me, I would still believe her because she has no reason to lie. I stood with her and was going to be by her side every step of the way. I told the detective that I didn't care what we had to do, I wanted to make sure that he would never hurt another child ever again.

As we began the whole process, I remember having a conversation with my best friend. Before we headed to court, I would always try to prepare myself to see his face and the fact that his family would come to support this monster really made me sick to my stomach. I didn't know what to think. I had so many mixed emotions, I didn't want people to pass on my child and treat her badly, but again I wanted him to fully pay for what he did.

Growing up, the older people would say, "What goes on in your house needs to stay in your house, don't put your business in the streets." There's so much wrong with that statement because if we choose to stay silent, that's how so many people get off hurting these babies because they are afraid of what this person or that person will say. And yes I worried about what people had to say, but at the end of the day, it was about my child. I didn't care what anybody had to say because people are going to talk regardless.

After it was all over, the District Attorney (DA) told us that she was one hundred percent sure that he would do it again within eight months and that this wasn't his first time doing it, but it was the first time someone pressed charges. I remember having a conversation with his mom the night that he was arrested, and her first question was, "Why didn't we talk about this before you pressed charges?"

There was no "I'm sorry" or anything, which made me believe what the DA had told us all the more. I would later receive a Facebook message from a girl asking me about a product I sell but really she wanted to let me know that one of her friends had gotten involved with the man and she thought he had molested her five-year-old niece. She wanted me and my daughter to talk with his girlfriend because she felt as if she was in danger.

I explained to her that we could talk but they would not talk to my child about anything. I was mad at the whole world. I felt for years that I was an unfit mother and that I let my kids down over and over. I asked myself how I let this happen. I had one job to do and that was to protect my kids, to make sure that nothing or nobody ever hurt them. I dropped the ball and that's something that I will deal with the rest of my life.

Forgiveness is something I had a really hard time with. I didn't want anybody preaching to me about forgiveness. I didn't want to hear it at all. I was mad and bitter to the point that I almost lost my mind. Nobody understood what I was dealing with. How could the one person who said they love you and wanted to spend the rest of their life with you hurt you like this?

Once again, I was broken and in a dark place. I had to find myself and learn who Dawanna was because everything the love that I had for people was gone. I didn't know who to trust or who I could talk to. I felt as if I was in this world by myself. I felt like God didn't love me. If he did, why would he allow this to happen? Why would he hurt my child like this?

So as time went on, God was the only one I could cry to late in the midnight hour and slowly but surely he restored me. Please don't get me wrong, this time around forgiveness was very hard. I work in a hospital, and it's hard to care for a patient that you know has done wrong to a child, but even then you have to do the right thing and pass the test. No, it's not easy but it's necessary to forgive so that you can let go of all that deadweight. Let it go!

What I didn't want from anybody was empathy. I just wanted my time to myself to try to figure out what was next., So at that moment all I could do was allow God to heal me. Yes, it took a lot of time, and what we feel is too hard and we can't get through it, but God is and will always be able.

What happened to my daughter took a big part of my life that day. I felt as if I died. It was almost as if I could not breathe. I felt like somebody was standing on my heart. The pain was so unbearable at that moment. I remember praying that God would allow something bad to happen to him for what he had done. I felt like I was stuck and didn't know how to get out of the hole that I was in. I felt that nobody understood what I was going though and that everywhere I went, people were talking about me and how I was a bad mother to allow something like this to happen to my child. I didn't want to go to work. I didn't want to do anything. I was depressed by what I went through, and because of that I went through it in silence. I didn't say anything to anybody as to how I was feeling, I thought that if I shared my feelings, people would judge me or that nobody would care.

It took years for me to let go of what happened to my daughter. As she started to heal and as I could see the change in her, it made me feel somewhat at peace and I started to feel better. As days and time went by I was able to let go and forgive. For a very long time, I was what you would call a made-up mess. I covered my wounds with my makeup, and I put a fake smile on my face to hide all the pain I was dealing with. The pain at times was unbelievable, I didn't know my own strength until that was all I had to depend on. Slowly but surely, I began to take the mask off. I began to allow my wounds to heal; and this time I allowed my wounds to heal for real. I had come to a place where I was sick, and I was so tired of hiding behind my pain. I started praying and asking God to allow me to let go of everything that was allowing me to stay in bondage, to allow me to fully heal, to no longer hurt and to stop hiding the pain. I was dead in the inside, I felt like I had nothing else left in me and I no longer wanted to feel this type of hurt., And just when I thought God didn't hear my prayers and he had forgotten about me, God restored me. That's why today I'm able to let people know that even when life hits, and it will hit, you can and will get through it. I had to pray like never before.

One of the first things that I had to do to start my healing journey was own it (accountability) . What could I have done differently? I asked myself a million questions. I had to learn to give myself some grace.

The second thing I had to do was forgive myself and realize that it was not my fault, he was just a sick individual that needed help.

The third thing I had to do was forgive everybody else. Forgiveness is not about erasing the past, but rather regaining control of your life and releasing resentment towards those who have wronged you. True forgiveness lies not in forgetting, but in taking back full control and letting go of any bitterness towards those that caused you pain.

I often tell people that we might bend but baby we won't break. They left me in the pit to die but God gave me a second wind. Just remember that there is life after the DROP! I SURVIVED THE DROP!

Utilize this space to journal and reflect. What are your thoughts after reading this chapter?

CHAPTER 6
Traditions of Release
Nichole Shoffner

In this chapter, I will speak about many different cleansing traditions to release negative energy. Some practices that I have tried or may be willing to learn more about or try while on my journey. I would like to discuss incorporating mindfulness and a few different ways you can learn meditation practices during your daily routine, while building a personal tradition of breaking generational curses that your family may encounter.

<u>Cleansing traditions to release negative energy</u>

I believe negative energy can attach to other people or may rub off on you. Meaning if you are around someone who is always negative, who never sees the good or positive in anything around them or who even speaks negatively all the time, their energy may transfer over to you.

There are many ways you can release negative energy from you or around your space. First, I would have to say, start with prayer. Prayer is communication with God. It helps you develop a relationship with God. When dealing with negative energy, you must stay prayed up to try to help the ones who are negative, but you cannot let someone with that type of energy drain you. If you can't help that person, you may have to let them go so they can seek the help they need to turn around their thought process. They will need to focus on themselves to overcome the negativity.

Promoting positivity is another way to release negative energy. You want to stay positive, think positively and speak positively. Read positive affirmations. By being positive, you help build a better mindset and clear mind. You can also visualize light. Light is always better than darkness. What helps me to clear away negative energy on a bad day or at the end of a rough week is a hot bath along with some breathing exercises, just to relax, clear my mind and gain peace of mind during that moment. I also enjoy burning my favorite scented candles during the times I feel as though I need to remove the negative energy off or away from me. This is a part of self-love or selfcare.

We need these moments to rejuvenate ourselves and not to continue to carry around the negative energy of being miserable. Some days may seem hard to promote self-care for yourself though, especially if you're a woman. Women wear multiple hats, constantly taking care of others. They may lose themselves and end up placing themselves on the back burner. Because making most of the sacrifices for your family may become overwhelming, you must incorporate some time for yourself. It will help with lowering stress and assist with a better healthier lifestyle.

Speaking from experience, I know what that feels like to be placed on the back burner. I'm trying to do better with providing more 'me' time for myself during the present and future.

Reading can be a beneficial tool in overcoming negative thoughts or depression. Reading to me is also good to keep your brain functioning. You are exercising your brain. Reading improves brain connectivity. It will also help your vocabulary comprehension, improve your concentration and help with your memory. If you don't enjoy reading books, take a few moments to read a newspaper or a magazine. I love to read a good book and get lost inside of it. It will have your mind so intrigued, you will want to find out what happens next.

If you are not into reading, learn a new hobby. You can learn how to play an instrument or how to start a garden. Along with what I've mentioned, you can attend a yoga class. If you are unable to go to a class, you can start at home by doing a few stretches along with some deep breathing. You may want to find a quiet place to sit and meditate. We'll talk more about that in the next section, but there are many ways to cleanse negative energy around your space.

Some also believe in saging their space or homes. Saging is a traditional technique coming from a Native American tradition of smudging. They believe when you sage your home, you are removing unwanted negative energy. Saging is recommended after a big change, a long period of illness or after having someone enter your home that brought negative energy into your home. This is a good process if someone would like to clear all of the negative energy in their space, home, work or self.

All these options will help release any negative energy you may be dealing with now so you can prepare yourself for the future.

<u>Incorporating mindfulness and meditation practices</u>

Meditation is a practice of mindfulness when you are focusing the mind on a particular object, thought, or activity to train attention, awareness and achieve a mentally clear and emotionally calm and stable state of mind. There are a few steps of mediation.

First, you must set your intention to meditate. The second step is to concentrate. The third step is insight. The longer we keep our focus on one idea, the more we will see or develop sensitivity, along with the three R's: we need to know when to recognize the issue you may be dealing with, come up with a resolution, we then must release any hurt, frustration or pain you may be holding on to. Once you have released all that you needed to release, then you may return to your peaceful place, especially in your heart. View the return as a fresh start at life. You can release and restart as many times as you are needed.

There is no limit to how many times you may have to reset in life. Release and return (reset) however many times you need to. In the end, just be sure you understand the three R's (Recognize, Release and Return), which can be a helpful tool throughout life.

Meditation can play a huge part in your life in cleansing negative energy from you, your home or workspace. It can assist with rewiring our brain and is a Biblical concept: Jesus used meditation to gain strength and discernment. Luke 6:12 tells us about the time Jesus went out to a mountainside to pray, meditate and spend the night praying to God. In Psalms, we are told to meditate on God's law and word day and night.

For me, I enjoy being near water to reset or let go of stress. When I'm near water, whether it is the ocean or a lake, it helps me focus and get my thoughts out clearer. I may plan my trip after midnight, and I will walk down to the water just to listen to God's work. Or I will get up extra early to catch the sunrise; or sit on the balcony to listen and drink my morning coffee. I always find myself getting lost in the waves. I breathe deeply while releasing any worries or anything I may have had on my mind before arriving. I look at the ocean as a spiritual cleaner, with the salt water for healing. take a moment to look at God's beautiful creation.

If I'm unable to be near water, I will play some ocean videos just to hear the relaxing sound of the waves. I also enjoy listening to the rain. Some people may get upset when it rains, I actually love it. The rain can also be relaxing and can be helpful on days you may want to meditate.

Being in nature can also be a big help. Maybe going on a nature walk, on a trail in your neighborhood, or sitting outside on a nice morning, having a cup of coffee while listening to the bird's chirp or the wind swaying can also be relaxing. You can use this for meditation. I've tried these listed and this practice has been very helpful to me and has assisted me in becoming a better version of me, just by allowing myself those few minutes out of the day.

Breathing exercises play a huge role while you are meditating. Taking a few moments to do some deep breathing and closing your eyes to meditate will help remove stress. You must be calm and relaxed during this state and allow your mind to be free.

Study shows meditation can heal your brain. It can strengthen the areas that are responsible for your memory, learning, attention and self-awareness. Practice can also help with calming down your nervous system. Over time, mindfulness meditation can increase your memory and attention. The difference between meditation and mindfulness is that meditation is a practice that reels in on our thoughts to calm the mind, while mindfulness requires us to be aware of what is around us and how our bodies feel.

1. Set aside some time.
2. Observe the present moment as it is.
3. Let your judgments roll by, treat it as a judgment-free zone.
4. Return to observing the present moment.
5. Be kind to your mind.

Stress can make it harder to enter a state of relaxation and focus during meditation or mindfulness. While we are currently living in stressful times, we must try to remember to find a quiet area with no distractions, whether in your home or elsewhere. The quiet area you have located is just for yourself. Now take some deep breaths, relax, release and let go of that stressful day or rough week you had.

One of the first mindful exercises is mindful breathing. It is allowing yourself to breathe in and out, but to also relax your mind and let go of anything negative or any worries you may be dealing with at that time.

While you are practicing mindfulness and meditation, do not forget other helpful techniques such as prayer. Starting with daily prayer assists you in building a closer relationship with God. It can also open your mind, body and soul to be able to see and think clearly.

Some people like to include yoga with their meditation. Yoga and meditation aim to quiet the mind in order to cultivate a deeper connection and understanding of self. They both teach you to tune into your breath, pay attention to bodily sensations and learn to accept reality as it is in that moment.

You would want to meditate after doing your yoga and breathing work. Participation in these activities has been linked to emotional well-being. They can be used to combat anxiety, depression and stress. Yoga would be a great goal to achieve in the near future, you may want to set a challenge for yourself to start learning about yoga. I have recently started learning about yoga and have tried it for my daily exercise. .

I have recently begun journaling. It is very helpful to write out your thoughts and helps with stress, anxiety and frustration. Whether you are happy, sad or mad, you should write so you are not carrying around the stress on your shoulders and you have a clear mind.

Building a personal tradition of breaking generational curses

Generational curses are an uncleansed iniquity that increases in strength from one generation to another. They are applied and maintained on three levels: genetic, environmental and supernatural. These can include addiction (drugs, alcohol, sex, etc.), mental illness (depression, schizophrenia, bipolar depression, etc.) and environmental (poverty, broken relationships, divorces, etc.). On a genetic level, it is important to understand that generational curses began with the fall of man in the garden of Eden.

> *The soul that sinneth, it shall die. The son shall not bear the iniquity of the father, neither shall the father bear the iniquity of the son: the righteousness of the righteous shall be upon him and the wickedness of the wicked shall be upon him. Ezekiel 18:20*

I can speak about my past experiences with a few of these topics. First mental illness is real and can be hereditary. I have a few family members who suffer from mental illness, myself included. It is difficult to understand what a person goes through when they are dealing with a mental illness. Two of my male cousins suffer from schizophrenia: one was born with his mental illness while the other cousin ended up being diagnosed with schizophrenia due to drug usage of PCP. I've watched them fight within themselves just to make it another day. This illness can take a toll on your mind and body. The sufferers may hear voices in their head telling them to do certain things. If their brain is not balanced with medication, they can be a danger to themselves or others around them who are not aware of their illness.

As a teen, I went to visit my older cousin in a mental institution. This was my first time in a psychiatric hospital, and I remember being scared, but walking down those halls to go to the visiting room was a game changer for life. I remember telling my aunt, "Wow, I've never seen so many young patients in a mental hospital before." I was always the type to not judge anyone and to try to see the good in everyone. And while visiting my cousin, some of those patients came up just to have a conversation. One of the nurses mentioned a few of them never had visits from their family. Hearing that made me sad inside. While I was there, I conversed with a few, I even played games with one patient. I didn't treat them differently or was no longer afraid because they were human just like me.

From that day forward, I always would thank God for a sound mind, because it could have been the other way around. I would advise if you haven't researched or learned anything about mental illness, educate yourself on the subject. It is very important that we take care of our mental health the same way we take care of everything else. You want a stable, clear mind.

"What goes on in my house, stays in my house." This phrase has caused a lot of families to have secrets, lies and abuse in the household. As a kid, I remember hearing that statement a lot. With our generation and family, we must do better than what our ancestors passed down from generation to generation. With future generations of our blood line to come, we must work hard at breaking generational curses and build generational wealth and generational blessings.

I believe one of the first steps to take is to have open and crucial conversations with your children. You want to provide a safe place for your kids, so that they will know and understand they can always have a relationship with their parents and will come to their parents to have those uncomfortable conversations, if needed. Try to always listen and keep the communication open.

Family personal business that should remain in the family household consists of hard financial situations and family disagreements. Some may also include being ashamed of family members due to mental illness. They may consist of alcohol, and drug addiction, incest, sexually assault or molestation by a family member and domestic violence in the household, just to name a few.

I experienced all I listed. Alcohol and drug addiction played a big part in destroying a few of my family members. Starting with my parents both dealt with their own demise, both were able to overcome the addiction. I even experienced my own addictions due to trying to self-medicate so that I did not have to deal with the hurt from my past. Not knowing my own addictions would or did lead me down a rabbit hole.

When you set out to speak your truth and tell your story, you may feel alone, embarrassed, ashamed, scared, not knowing where to start. You may also end up dealing with depression, anxiety and constantly wanting to isolate yourself from everyone in the world due to fear of the reaction you may receive from people who do not know or understand your truth. For me and my truth, it is still a daily battle, or I should say, it still bothers me even now as an adult woman. Being molested, raped, and dealing with domestic violence or any type of trauma takes time to heal. When you have had to endure so much hurt and pain at a young age, the result is a lot of self-doubt and insecurities; and you may deal with depression in life.

At the age of eight, my parents divorced, and I remember we were in my mom's first apartment afterward. It seems like that was when life really took downward a turn of events. There were many times I felt alone; like I had no one to talk to about my darkest, deep secrets or certain things I went through growing up as a kid. I didn't want to feel like I was being judged or made out to be a liar.

It doesn't help the fact that when I was five years old, I was molested by a family member. I was told by one of the women in my family that I, as a young child, was lying and that her son would "never" do anything like that. Being told that you're lying about something you had no control over or knew nothing about until that day was hurtful, especially coming from the woman who taught you how to pray and how to be a young lady. I was a kid and as a kid, my innocence was stolen from me. During those years and even now, I felt like the outcast or the black sheep in my family. I hated to go to family functions just because I would have to face the one who had violated me. I tried to avoid him every minute I was around him because he acted like nothing ever happened to me.

Then six or seven years later, I was molested again for the second time. This time it was by a stranger to me, but a friend of my mother. I woke up out of my sleep with a random stranger on top of me, his hand over my mouth so I couldn't scream. I remember him being so heavy on me that I could barely move. My heart was beating so fast, because I thought I was having a nightmare. I tried to fight him off of me, but I wasn't strong enough. He told me to shut up before he did what he was doing to me to my little sister, who shared a bed with me and was asleep. She was around the age of nine at that time, I had just turned twelve. I kept quiet to protect my sister because I didn't want anything to happen to her. I remember laying there in the dark thinking, "Damn, where is my mom? And why hasn't she come into my room or up the hallway or something by now?" My mom was out at the store or fighting her addiction habits at that time, while I was home in my bedroom being molested in what was supposed to have been my safe place.

I let my mom know what had occurred as soon as I heard her come through the door. I called her to my room, and she handled that situation right away. Later on that same year, after school, I was raped by someone I went to school with. But due to what I had already endured, I never told a soul.

With me going through those different traumatic situations at such a young age, it made me not trust men. By the time I was a teenager, I was promiscuous. I didn't understand why I thought or felt the way that I did. Looking back on it today, I should have received some type of therapy. I didn't love myself; I didn't understand the value of my life or that my body was a temple, and I slipped into depression. I was great at hiding it around friends or family. At twelve, I dealt with suicide thoughts, and no one ever knew. I kept those thoughts to myself because I didn't want anyone to judge me or think I was crazy. I wasn't crazy, I was just hurt from keeping the pain inside me. I felt like no one would even notice if I wasn't here. I had no support, no one to depend on because I also had younger sisters I was looking after who looked up to me. I did whatever I had to do to make sure we ate, had clean clothes if my mom wasn't able to wash and that we were okay during our rough times. I tried to make it easier for my little sisters so they wouldn't be able to tell if we were going through a rough moment.

As an adult now, I understand both of my parents did the best they could with the hand they were dealt. Both experienced things in life that, at the time, may not have led to the best decisions then but some of their decisions made me and my sisters strong. Strong individuals who know how to survive. I remember at times asking God why this was my life, why this was happening to me or my family. I would even ask God if he heard my prayers because I felt like my prayers weren't being heard or answered. And if he did hear my prayers, why nothing was changing with our situation. I didn't know then not to question God. I was a teenager. Now I understand and know everything happens for a reason and even though we went through rough times, God kept us, protected us, and provided for us. I know from life experiences those dark days will have you viewing life differently or wanting to ask God a question or two.

As a young child, I didn't think I would make it to the age of twenty-one or adulthood, due to life choices and dealing with so many different struggles. When you are face-to-face with the demons that hurt you, you must find ways to cope and move forward in life. In order to break those types of generational curses, you must face the challenges head on. I wish I could have told myself some of this exact advice growing up. I needed to be saved, and to feel safe and protected. I learned at an early age how good God was. That is when my personal relationship with God started. I would pray or pray as best as I knew how at that age, not knowing how these next few months or years to come were going to turn out.

Every time I had to face a test in life, I felt overwhelmed. I didn't understand why I was going through so much. And it seemed like the more I prayed, the more I would be tested. Dealing with so much, my Sundays became silent. I became distant from everyone, and my heart was feeling weak. Once I had my children, I was able to feel love and I knew God was real and was good because he had blessed me with the greatest two blessings: my daughter and my son. I knew they were the blessings I needed in my life to move forward. This was when I started releasing and letting go of a lot of the hurt I had experienced when I had my children. I buried it deep down inside.

From the time I carried my children in my womb, I would talk to them, and promise them that I would try my hardest to break any generational curses in my family by providing open communication, teaching them how to pray and to have a relationship with God. I prepared myself to have hard conversations with them both. At an early age, I taught them both about good and bad touches. I made sure they understood the difference. Having those conversations with my children allowed my daughter and son to feel more comfortable speaking to me about anything. I let my children know to never be afraid to come to me. With my past experiences, I believe the earlier you have those conversations with your children (if they are old enough to understand), the better. Trust your children and trust yourself that you raised your kids the correct way. Keep an open-door policy so when or if that day comes, you will be prepared to have those conversations with your children, and they will feel safe coming to you and no one else.

We, as a family or a "village" in our community, must protect our youth, our children. That includes your nieces, nephews, God-children, neighbor children and even random children you may cross paths within the world. Be selective about who you have around your children. It's sad to say, but also pay attention to family members. Not everyone has good intentions. A child may be taught to lie due to fear, but they might not do so convincingly. Notice or look at the body language, this will tell you if they are going through stress or a bad situation. There are always signs in children. They can sense the good or bad in people. Most importantly, listen to the child. If they state something has happened to them or they have seen certain things, please believe them.

Also seek therapy. In our communities and families, a lot of us were taught to hold our feelings and emotions in or pray about it and move on. You didn't hear too much about going to see a therapist or having a therapy session. I feel therapy would have been very beneficial to me as a young child and teenager. Without therapy, I held on to a lot of hurt which made me become overprotective of my children when they were little. I still deal with certain trust issues and anxiety to a certain extent. Don't be afraid or embarrassed to seek therapeutic help.

In my family, there are generational curses in marriage. Most marriages in my family haven't lasted. My grandparents were married over thirty years before my grandpa passed but most of my other family members who were married have now divorced except for a few. Even my parents divorced when I was younger. As for myself, I've never been married. I always wanted to be married. It just hasn't happened the way I planned or hoped.

I come from a family of strong women. Some of us have to allow the man to lead and provide for his family, meaning we may have to compromise and be submissive in certain situations to continue being the modern-day married woman we would like to be. Women in our culture have been told, "You don't need a man to survive." This has come from everyday society, family, friends, or even maybe the government. Also, I understand some marriages do not work. But sons and daughters need their father in their life one hundred percent, not just sometimes.

Domestic violence can be a generational curse and can be passed down hereditarily to the next generation. One out of three women will experience some sort of domestic violence situation throughout their lifetime. When children are young, their minds are like sponges, soaking up everything. If a child has witnessed domestic violence, it can be traumatizing. If a young boy witnesses a situation, he may grow up to think it is okay to become physical, aggressive, or verbally abusive towards the women in their life. If a young girl witnesses a situation, young girls will think it is okay to be hit on or spoken to aggressively because they might have witnessed their mom, or a family member endure domestic violence, thinking that is a part of being loved. That is not love.

I myself experienced and survived a few domestic violence relationships all at different stages of my life. Even though I fought back or would try to fight back, my actions would only make the situation worse. I want young girls, young boys, women and men to know that love is patient, love is kind. Love does not bring hurt and pain from physical abuse. Know your worth. Understand the red flags and know you are no one's punching bag and it is not your fault. You are not to blame yourself. A man who hits a woman is a coward and is dealing with his own trauma or insecurities that he needs to seek help for. Love yourself enough to know when to walk away. You deserve better.

We have to break those generational curses of abuse. This includes physical, verbal or mental abuse. All of these stages of abuse can be very damaging. Fifty percent of the women in these situations are strong enough to leave, cut ties and seek help. The other fifty of women in domestic violence situations will not be so lucky. Due to all the abuse breaking the woman down mentally each day, she will eventually lose the fight and may even lose her life from fighting back or attempting suicide to escape the reality of the hurt and pain. I would say I was a lucky one, by the grace of God. Even though I escaped my situations physically doesn't mean I was free and at peace mentally.

The best thing in life that is free is your peace. Having peace in your home is a blessing. No one can alter your peace unless you allow it. It has taken me a while to gain the peace I needed and was searching for so long. I allowed God to handle my battles while I put all of my faith in him. All we need is faith the size of a mustard seed and God will handle the rest.

I feel like at this stage in my life, I can finally start to breathe easier than I did before. Out of every dark moment in my past, I knew God was good and had a plan for me. I knew I was destined to see the light and finally no more dark days. I still have my challenges, but not how I used to be. I had to learn how to accept forgiveness. You are not forgiving the ones that have hurt you for their sake, but for yours, so that you're able to move on. Honestly, I'm still working on making progress in one area, but I have determined it will no longer hinder me or hold me back. I have realized, in life you may go through different situations and life may not be easy, but those tests will only make you a stronger person. You must put in the work to become a better person. Take all of the hurt, pain, and anger and turn it into a positive outcome.

It took me some time to understand that process. As my mentor and close friend of mine shared with me, I had to change my mindset. I had to start thinking and speaking positively. The best advice she ever provided to me has been helping me along the way. There is power in the tongue. So before speaking now, I try to take a moment to think first. Each day for me moving forward has been a work in progress. I also understand, James 2:26, "Faith without work is dead." I continue to pray daily to keep my faith strong with God. I'm learning that what God has for me, is for me. I will continue to give God all of my worries, hurt, pain and anger because he is the only one that will see me through.

I wasted so much time over the years trying to do things "my way" when I should have been giving it all to God then. I'm sure I made him laugh a few times by trying it my way and telling him my plans.

I have overcome depression, molestation, sexual assault, domestic violence and am still working on fear. I continue to work on myself using different techniques to control or assist with my anxiety. I still have a lot to work on. I'm ready to walk in my journey and continue to face each challenge that may come against me or the goals I set out to achieve for myself. I have survived the good, bad, and the ugly pain. And even though it was hard, I survived. I made it through and will continue to make it through.

In closing, break those chains of abuse, molestation, addiction. Break those generational curses. It has to start somewhere to see better in your family. Set goals to promote generational wealth and goals to rise above poverty. Set morals, along with positive solutions, with your children. Learn how to say no sometimes; it is okay to say no. Do not feel guilty. Do not feel guilty for providing self-care and self-love for yourself. If you are like me and constantly give and don't take care of yourself first, one day there may not be much more to give. Also know that the test you may have been given can be a blessing in disguise. Continue to fight forward to break family generational curses. And remember forgiveness is the key. You must forgive yourself to let all of the bad, negative things go, to be able to move forward and not to carry a heavy burden on your heart. Continue to think positive, speak positive, it will change your thought process for the better you.

Utilize this space to journal and reflect. What are your thoughts after reading this chapter?

CHAPTER 7
Intergenerational Healing
Shani'ya Faucette

Trouble breathing, nausea, cramps and dizziness. These are some symptoms of poison. What exactly is poison? Poisoning is causing harm to a person by putting something harmful in or towards a person. In this chapter, I want to help shine light on the things that are silently killing our communities of people.

Relationships, interactions, and activities involving multiple generations. This is what intergenerational means in proper terms. In simple terms, generational fits perfectly here. Have you ever experienced not being heard because of age differences? Being told to stay quiet because whatever the oldest person says goes? Due to intergenerational trauma, many of us are left scared. Bruised. Feeling alone within your own family or culture. Intergenerational trauma plays a crucial role in shaping us into the people we are today.

Do not get me wrong, there are positive aspects, like the passing down of wisdom, but some of the things that were passed down have caused a continuation of hurt. We developed certain mindsets, beliefs, and behaviors from these intergenerational experiences that we sometimes subconsciously pass on down the line. I am here to help you identify some of these connections and offer ways that you can heal from them.

Genocide is a key factor in most cultures' trauma. Our ancestors experienced genocide which contributes to a lot survival mentality. Learning how to survive is a great skill to have to be able to press forward in times of battle. However, being in a constant state of survival is not healthy for even the strongest person. It can cause you to become anxious, to not reserve your energy, and to constantly be withheld from your fullest potential.

What happens when you become fluent in survival and nothing else? You become a person who is always on guard.

You hold on tight to things you should let go of instead of seeking better. You're less likely to receive help because you're used to being dropped by others. Surviving is like a hand tightly wrapped around your neck awaiting the moment of your last breath. It's feeling like you are drowning, while fighting so hard to live. Walking on glass, screaming for help, heart torn in two. It is faking it until you make it. Smiling when it hurts. Laughing instead of crying. Shedding blood but life still goes on.

Life comes with the need to survive, highs, and lows. The high is when you forget about all your problems and fears. You live life in the moment with no regrets. You're filled with joy, and you feel like you're on Cloud Nine. Highs are like a drug that keeps you feening for the good times.

The lows hurt and sometimes it leaves you speechless. They make the highs look unreachable, yet the lows are so teachable. Lessons learned.

Life is a journey of surviving, highs, and lows. A lot of these moments can at times point back to our intergenerational trauma or generational curse. Make the very best of the life you're given and fight till it's finished.

I myself have had my run in with survival, the highs, the lows, and battling generational curses. I fluctuate between the four, and every day is different from the other. I have survived abuse both physical and emotional. The main thing I have struggled with and is a part of the curse is silence. This is now the time to reject silence and let your voice be heard. The most powerful thing you can do for yourself is heal from intergenerational curses.

There are several important steps concerning healing. The first one is acknowledgement. In order to acknowledge effectively, you need to be intentional. Find a place to yourself away from others where you can decompress. For me, my quiet place is always my car, I can listen to music, take a drive, sing, pray, whatever I need to do. It is important that you find your space or create a comforting environment.

I didn't grow up hearing about healing. Mental health was never talked about within my community growing up, that was unheard of. We were told for generations to basically suck it up and keep on moving. But we now live in a time where there are endless resources available to us, and I am here to assure you that it is okay to not be okay and to seek professional help. Avoid people that will judge you shedding light on the things that have held you bound. Family, friend, or stranger denied access. Blood does not give you a right, titles are earned. I remember times when I would share certain things only to be told I was just "looking for attention", or ignored, unnoticed. We have to let go of these toxic sayings or practices that have been passed down from generation to generation. Truth be told, we are the very people killing each other, mentally and emotionally. Children are taught to be seen and not heard, to not have questions, and to go with whatever an adult says. We are setting children up to be taken advantage of because their voices are being snatched away from them. I know because my voice was snatched from me. I went through physical, emotional, and sexual abuse at very young age for a span of years. The one thing I would tell my younger self is speak up, fight back, and never stop shining. So now I echo to you, speak up, fight back, and never stop shining!

Allow yourself time and be easy on yourself. Healing takes a lot of time, hard work, and dedication. Especially if this is your first encounter with true healing, you must grant yourself grace. Healing looks different person to person. Be careful not to compare yourself to a journey that is not your own. I struggled with this step for a long time. I would get angry with myself, I felt like I was delaying myself. Growing up, I felt like everything was fast paced, any demand had to be done then and there. As I have gotten older I have developed the toxic trait of getting things done when I get around to it. This is because my motivation plummeted a lot after the sexual abuse I encountered. I am still working at building my tolerance back up and not living like a zombie for the rest of my life. That is a part of the process, acknowledging the ugly things about yourself and forming a plan to work towards a goal. All these things come with time no matter what the target is. Time allows you to really think about and reflect over your life. With enough thinking and self-reflection, you will get to the root of your issue. Think about a tree and how a tree that has been standing 20+ years you can imagine is large in size. Due to the age and size of that tree, it is deeply rooted in the ground. One root makes room for others to grow over time. That is the same with intergenerational curses. They become a part of our tree, sucking the life day by day, eventually leaving us with dead branches. Getting to the root of your issue can save your life, in the sense of becoming free.

The second step is having support. This journey is not an easy one and you need people to lean on, to push you when you are feeling too weak to push yourself. Take a look around, families gossip about each other, hate, avoid, and sometimes do not even claim each other. This is another cycle that needs to be broken. It should always be us against the problem and never us against each other. If we could learn that we are more powerful together rather than being against each other, we could accomplish more than we ever have. Find your support partner and lean on them when the going gets rough, and always be sure to support them as well.

Healthy relationships can really be key in this process. Again, family dynamics are typically broken. We usually have a falling out with a person and never speak with them. This is another one of those toxic traits we continue to pass down the line. To have a true support team, good rapport is good to have.

Mending together the broken pieces as a family can be tremendous in the healing process.

I too am on a journey and the going has not been easy. I had to ask myself, if you were not you would you be cool with you? At that time, I said no. Healing seemed too hard, but I am here to tell you that it is not too hard but well worth it. I had a sense of fear when it came to healing. A part of my generational poison was people pleasing. Always worried about what people may say or what people may think. I have faced bouts of financial stress, a poison that has become the norm within the community. I cannot settle or stand for anything less than generational wealth.

This journey is a mindset. If you never change your way of thinking, then you will remain stuck in the same cycle. It's typical to grab a hold of the short term or the easier path rather than taking the longer term. If you truly want to be free, you must make up in your mind exactly what that looks like to you, be firm and stand strong. With all things, do them with a sincere and loving heart and the rest falls in place. Uphold your end of the deal, give it go, and let the rest follow.

Oftentimes in the healing process, it can be helpful to rekindle your spiritual connections. I know someone who can help put you back together if you let him. He can order your steps in the way that they should go. He can love you back to life. He will be there with you when you fall and help to pick you back up. This is someone who is always there for you when friends or family are not there. That someone is God. Allow him to put you back together. To fill you, to make you over again. This life goes too rough without the Lord.

Always remember exactly where your help comes from. Rebuilding your spiritual connection can be the source of your strength. There is always light at the end of the tunnel. When it gets hard, keep fighting and remember that you can do all things through Christ who strengthens you. When your back is against the wall, remember the Lord invites you to cast all your cares upon him. If you feel like it is too late for you, that is a lie. If you have breath in your body, obey God. If you feel like you are unworthy of His love, He loves you with an everlasting love. If you feel like He does not hear you, then get on your face and cry out, until you feel the presence of your Father.

One positive thing passed down from generations is having faith in God. I am truly thankful to have grown up in church because it has played an integral part in my healing process. There were times when I would feel lonely or afraid, the one thing I did know how to do was pray and seek my Father. My comfort is housed with the Lord, and I know that I have unlimited access to that comfort. When the going gets a little rough, I know I can lean on God in my times of need.

I also had to pair this with letting go of patterns. I found myself becoming bitter, something that happens all too often in our community. For me, my pattern was shutting down. I don't like talking to people, being around people, or allowing people to touch me. I have, in a sense, developed a guard. I have been working on this for some time now though and have made good improvements. For the most part, I prefer to stay to myself, but I gradually made myself accessible to the ones that should be allowed in. Healing protects you and if that means guarding or secluding yourself for a period of time, then take the necessary precautions. Discovering and addressing your patterns will be extremely helpful in the journey of healing. It can prevent a lot of moving in circles or doubling back.

As mentioned previously, it is okay to seek professional help! After going through molestation for a span of years and my family finding out later, therapy was suggested to me as a resource to help me, but I immediately shut it down. I think I did this because I wanted to run away. I wanted everyone to believe that I was okay. I put on a brave face when I was in front of others, and avoided everyone that I could when I was able.

I also never heard much about therapy, nor was I taught on the importance of therapy. I felt like I had been battling in silence for so long that everyone was just scrambling to fix me. I felt like a charity case, and I shut down. To this day, in all transparency, that is a scar that I have not fully addressed. It just feels easier to leave it as is, but that is not healthy. I have written out a plan and I have described what that area of healing looks like for me. I encourage and challenge you too to address that deep hurt and do not let it consume you.

Deep hurt is something that will linger for a long period of time, it can knock you to your feet and leave you there. It can be generationally passed down, which is unfortunate, but the curse stops here. Deep hurt can cloud your mind and keep you focused on the pain or the negatives instead of the joys of life. A lot of the generational hurt is passed down because of this. Hurt people hurt people, sometimes not even intentionally. This is why intergenerational healing is important. If you press on without taking care of these things, you wind up being the same person that people have been to you, hurting everyone who crosses your path.

Another thing linked to deep hurt that we do not typically think about is sickness. Deep hurt comes with sadness, anger, stress, or many other negative emotions. Too much of this can cause you to become physically ill. High stress levels can cause your blood pressure to rise, and many other things. Just like the symptoms of poison, you can become nauseous, fatigued, or have disrupted sleep patterns. When I am under stress, it becomes hard for me to sleep well at night, and if you do not get enough sleep, it all becomes a domino effect. These are the times that my spiritual connection has become helpful, when the weight becomes too heavy, and I know that I can lean on my Father.

You create the narrative this time around. Do not live the narrative that was given to you. We are done being programmed. Go to work. Go home. Go to school. Go home. Go to church. Go home. Repeat. I have woken up to the equation we have been sold our entire life.

The one thing that I want to see more of is black generational wealth. My family has accomplished much for sure but there has been more blood, sweat, and tears than gain. I am twenty-two years old, and I refuse to live my life by this narrative given to us. Go to grade school, go to college and owe thousands of dollars, and then work for them your entire life only to die and not get the chance to taste and see. We are taught to hold onto your money with a tight grip. Though that is correct, you should absolutely save. However, that money is not growing, it is sitting, and it cannot go with you when you go. It is time to start investing in your future and the generations after you.

I have learned it is not about the business you can produce; it is about learning a skill or skills and gaining from them. A business can fail easily if you do not take the time to build the skill. The top categories to build skills in are sales, editing, marketing, and real estate. These first three are what can get you the last one. Sales are good because people are always looking for something to buy. The key is finding something that is in extremely high demand or something that grabs the attention of your audience. Do you know how many people have come up off something as simple as eyelashes that we were already born with? A ton. If you have an idea for sales, get the ball rolling!

Editing has a high demand now. With content creation being a huge thing right now, if you develop skills in editing videos or pictures, there is financial gain there.

Marketing is something you need as a business and offers a lot of room to succeed.

Lastly, people will always need shelter and if you can provide it, you are in the game. Airbnb has become huge in the past few years and is a great investment. What I suggest is to start with sales, editing, or marketing, and whatever you generate from these skills, let it pay for the property. Once the property is obtained, allow it to pay for another property and so on while still keeping that stream of income from one of the original three. Financial freedom or literacy is rarely obtained in the black community, but that curse stops here. Do your research as I have done extensive amounts of research. It will not be easy but nothing good in life comes easy.

You and I can break the cycle of trauma, pain, and negative patterns that have been passed down through generations. Allow yourself to snatch your voice back firmly, so that you are able to share your story and help your sisters and brothers. Sharing your story helps to break the cycle that our ancestors did not have the opportunity to do. Foster a deep understanding of your family background and or history and this can be pivotal in navigating your journey. Communicate with those connected to you about your journey and how you need or want to be supported. Look into therapeutic resources to help you along the way. I encourage everyone battling deep hurt to at least try to seek professional help, and if it turns out it is not for you, then that is okay! Remember to be easy on yourself through this process! It will not be easy, but it will be worth the fight in the end.

This is what I like to call choosing your pain. Would you rather experience some short term hurt that will set you up for freedom, or stay bound and carry long term hurt forever? Regardless of what I or anyone around you thinks, it only matters if you truly want to heal yourself. That is something I had to come to terms with, at a fairly young age. Everyone around me wanted to fix me, but that did no good because at that time I did not want to fix me. I never noticed the weight I was carrying until I got into my twenties and the twenties started hitting hard at the beginning stages!

I am proud of myself for embarking on the journey of healing, though I still have a long way to go. I have never been in a better place emotionally than I am now. I want that for you too! Know that someone out there believes in you, and you are loved! You are not in this battle by yourself! Allow your support in and cancel the curses together. Here's to being the curse breakers.

Utilize this space to journal and reflect. What are your thoughts after reading this chapter?

CHAPTER 8
Embracing Positive Change
Dr. Karon Graves

There are layers to me that I, at times, struggle to understand. As I try to think back about when it started, I find there are parts of the subconscious tucked away. There are so many memories, that when reflected upon brew a number of emotions and feelings from uncomfortable to smiles. However, in recent years, it was clear that my journey towards healing must begin in order to experience greatness and truly embrace the necessary changes required to fulfill my purpose.

Growing up, I was constantly trying to fit in and understand what was "normal" or "acceptable" by society's standards. This led to feelings of being an outsider and constantly struggling to find my place with society and even relationships. Over the years, I started to question why I was trying so hard to conform and began to realize that I needed to embrace my unique identity and experiences in order to truly be happy. It has and continues to be a journey of self-discovery and self-acceptance, which by no means has been easy. However, by examining my past and understanding how it shaped beliefs, views and my character, I was able to let go of society's expectations and embrace positive change. I learned to see myself not as a stranger in a foreign land, but as an individual with a rich and diverse background. This allowed me to imagine a future filled with possibilities and to embrace change with open arms and without worry. It takes courage and self-reflection, but when you let go of the need to fit in and instead embrace who you truly are, positive change becomes a natural and exciting part of life.

It was not an easy process. I had to confront my fears and insecurities. I had to learn to let go of the idea and concept of how "normal" or "acceptable" is considered. I had to break free from the constraints of societal pressures, expectations, and illusions. I continue to be destined and determined to find my own path. I have found the journey towards self-discovery and self-acceptance to be challenging at times. In trying to understand my life and the goals of becoming a better version of myself, the need to examine things in my past necessitated confrontation, no matter how uncomfortable it felt. I had to be real and transparent with myself to examine everything and in order to move forward, a closer look at my foundation and roots was necessary . Those connections that helped to build and shape me into the woman I am today.

If I listen closely enough, there is still a small voice I hear internally saying, "You better get up and do the best that you can." I can hear the ringing in my ears. Those words, that voice, my grandmother's favorite saying, "Do the best you can." One of the last videos I have of her before she lost her voice and passed away was that message. From her hospital bed, she still managed to send a message of hope: regardless of what trials come, keep going.

How did I develop a level of resilience despite all of the adversity? My parents were teenagers who had no clue how to raise a child. However, they did the best they could to provide the love and nurturing necessary to see me through life. What in the world would a seventeen-year-old do with a child? How could a child who is barely mature be able to raise someone? How could a child be able to love a child? How could this young mother provide for anyone's needs? Would she be able to protect her? Would this be a generational curse of young parenthood? As I pondered these questions and thoughts, it dawned on me that my grandmother was, at the time of her first child's birth, barely fifteen years-old herself.

When I think about my relationship with my parents, specifically my mother, it becomes equally important to think about the relationships throughout the lineage, important to consider the relationships that stem back through the generations. As a young child growing up, I often wondered about the relationship between not only my grandmother and my mother but also what the relationship between my grandmother and her mother was. I learned that I came from a family of very strong women who were determined to make a difference, women determined to do what needed to be done by any means necessary, despite their youth.

My "Granny" Joyce was born in Barbados, which is actually the place of my birth. My grandmother desired better for her family and every decision she made was to ensure opportunities for future generations. Like most people growing up in the West Indies under British rule, there were certain trades that were specific to women of her era in the 1940-1970's. My grandmother's basic education consisted of training on caretaker and housekeeping duties. The goal was that young women in the islands would grow up and migrate to the United States or England to work for wealthy white families. The reality of this rite of passage came in 1971 when my grandmother set off to the United States of America and landed in New York, leaving behind my aunt, mother, and uncle. My entrance into this world would arrive the following year. It's amazing the decisions that women often have to make when it comes to their children. One could only suspect that the decision to venture out into a different world in order to create a better life was the first step that broke the generational curses of bondage in a country with the hopes of providing a better life for her family and future generations to come.

As someone who was born in a different country and migrated to the United States, I know that nothing is simply handed to you. The challenges and expectations are different, making the drive to achieve success even stronger. It is truly inspiring to see how my grandmother, who came to the United States as a housekeeper, blazed a trail for many others. She selflessly reached out and helped countless individuals multiple times. Watching both my mother and grandmother in the roles of caretakers for wealthy families while trying to live their dream became a natural innate instinct. The seeds and need for self-improvement were planted early on.

So, becoming a teenage parent would not be my story. Although I was not a teenager when I experienced my first pregnancy, the fear of the unknown and being a disappointment to my family led me to make decisions and choices that left deep-rooted scars and took me years to overcome.

Often, I wondered about the relationship between my grandmother and mother and what hidden secrets she kept hidden away. The best way to describe her would be God-fearing, humble, observant, quiet firecracker who was dedicated and loved her family. She often enjoyed sharing stories about her childhood and growing up. I don't really recall much about her mother apart from the complications she experienced and her loss of several children.

Which leads me to reflect on the relationship between my mother and myself. I often wondered about why there were days where I wanted affection, but I couldn't seem to reach her. There were days where my mother's eyes seemed to be just filled with so much sadness. What secrets was she holding that she couldn't share? Why did it seem to be so challenging for her to love my grandmother in such a way that I felt she needed to be loved when her memories started to fail?

There were so many things I didn't understand about this dynamic but one thing for sure was that when I became a mother, the life of my children would be much different, and they would be surrounded with expressions of love. Teaching my children how to embrace and accept love would become the mission and they would hear it daily.

I recall a few times when my mother would be so upset and so angry that I blamed myself for robbing her of her childhood. Was I the one at fault? Because of me, her childhood had escaped her. What child has the thoughts and feelings that if only their mother had the time or the opportunity to enjoy her childhood, things could be different? My mother was my protector, and I was hers but the fear of showing love to the future generation would have to change!

For several years, life consisted of long bus trips on the Greyhound Bus with my mother to visit my father who, at the time, lived in another country. My father had migrated to Canada from Barbados. We were in two different countries. Although I was a young child, it was clear that my mother had so much love for my dad that she would board the Greyhound Bus every weekend from New York and take me with her to visit Father.

My father was entirely the opposite of my mother. He was serious, stern, hardworking and authoritative. Silence would enter the room when he would walk in. The feelings of nervousness and being scared would just take over. He had this look of "try me." In time, I learned that his demeanor scared more than just myself. The intensity of his personality in many ways impacted my mother's happiness. She tolerated a lot and in many ways, it shaped my perspective about relationships, love, commitment, and who I am as a woman. These early interactions have molded and made me into the woman, the mother, the daughter, the sister, and the wife that I am today. It was the fracture in this bond that would shape my lens. It's not blame but the reality of the fibers that have shaped who I am and the need to shift the future.

My father was one of thirteen children and fell somewhere in the middle in terms of his birth order. He had several older siblings who I would never meet due to being raised in another country. Listening to the stories of how at least three of my father's older siblings chose to migrate to England always seemed to amaze me as I wondered what life was like for them. While two of his sisters migrated to Canada, the remainder of his siblings stayed behind in Barbados. I can't imagine how my grandmother must have felt separating from several of her children and sending them off for the opportunities for a better life. The others that remained would continue to revel in the traditions and culture of my birth country.

The hard choices that many West Indian parents and children had to make in order to survive and have a better life came at a far greater price than I ever wanted to experience.

My childhood wasn't easy. There were times when I would often wonder what my life would be if my parents were different. I watched how my mother would just take mediocre jobs. It was difficult because she was the smartest woman in the world in my eyes, beautiful, and deserving of much more.

The Importance of Education

What could I do differently to take it to the next level? It had to begin with not only obtaining a higher education but working harder to defy all of the odds that were stacked against me.

I don't remember the age I was when I realized my father could not read. I had spent days as a young child going to him asking him to read me a story and remember him looking at the pages of the book. I guess because I was a young child and unable to read myself, I never realized that the stories he told me were based on his imagination. When my father's inability to read became clear, the determination for education and to push myself to succeed became much greater. I recall the stories about him having to learn how to work the farm and at the tender age of ten having the responsibility of adulthood along with many of his siblings. What was evident was learning to use your hands and the need for survival through the use of learned skills exceeded the formal need for education. I can only imagine his struggle and stress of navigating in a world where reading was fundamental and paramount for understanding and negotiating key factors of life.

When I was in high school, I remember receiving notification that I had been selected to be a participant in a group called "Great Potential." I recall on my first day of sitting in the room with other selected individuals that they had all looked like me. But in front of this group of predominantly young, minority individuals was everyone who didn't look like us as they began to pitch the program. The days of skipping classes had finally caught up as we were told we had the potential to achieve academic greatness but were not meeting the mark for success. In my mind, I took everything that was said and made it a challenge to show otherwise. A level of greater determination arose in me as it became clear that my grandmother, followed by my mother, did not migrate to the United States as housekeepers for me to throw my education away and housekeeping to become my destiny. Something needed to change, and that moment was when I realized thinking differently about my future was necessary.

Academic success provided options that my parents and grandparents did not obtain. Simply graduating from high school was not enough. Working a minimum wage job was not enough. Learning to master my education became my dream. Each course completed successfully became the motivation to keep going. The BA pushed me to the MA which inspired me to work towards a PhD. I recall my father saying, at this stage, having too much education will make a person crazy. This would not be my story, but in that moment, it became clear that we can only think beyond the basics when taught.

Surviving Divorce

Throughout childhood, I watched how my mother endured so much. I watched how she would cry and fight back. I watched wishing that I had the inner strength to jump in and help. On one occasion, I remember living in our first-floor apartment, and my mother screaming to the top of her lungs as my father hit her with the broom. I remember my trying to jump on him and pull him away from her and getting knocked to the ground. I recall the look in his eyes as he turned to me and said, "Don't you ever put your hands on me." It was amazing to watch how my mother would bounce back and continue to push through after each encounter. My heart would ache, and a level of resentment grew. My father's anger was directed at my mother and in time, turned to me which led to me running away from home on a few occasions. It did not matter what was said and no questions were never asked before the belt would strike.

The depths of each slap and hit left scars that have yet to heal. The roots planted by my father led to me look at my first marriage differently, as I struggled to understand what kept my mother in her marriage to my father. Not only did I get married in my early twenties, it was clear and evident that my heart could not connect. I could no longer remain in my first marriage and find self-worth. I struggled for thirteen years to find my way out based on the pressure to please and not to disappoint. When I finally decided to become brave enough to walk away, another chain was broken in continuing to live a life of unhappiness.

I was coming out of an eighteen-year marriage and had three children who were depending on me. I was not allowed to quit. I was not allowed to give up. I was wondering how in the world I was going to make it. There was nothing about the dissolution of a marriage that I saw as positive. It felt as though

I had experienced a death, a loss; and I carried every emotion that went along with grief. I found myself asking questions about the meaning of true love and even more, what was wrong with me? Why? How did I grow out of love/care? Was it really love to begin with, or was it filling an empty space from my first love many years ago? Did I even love myself? Did I know myself? I remember saying that I would not remain stuck in making other people happy when I felt as though my soul was dying. I felt pieces of myself chipping away at the years and tried so hard to hold on. There were days of crying, but no one saw my tears or heard my cry.

But this is what you prayed for, this is what you wanted, or so you thought.

How long do you walk on a rug before learning that the bounce no longer exists? How do I break the news to my children? How do I tell them? How do I tell my family? After all, over the years I watched women model "fake it till you make it" with such grace. I had just turned forty but faking it was no longer a place of comfort.
Lord, what am I to learn? This was no longer healthy for me, and change was needed.

I can't say that I wasn't inspired by my aunt who had been married for over thirty years or my ex-mother-in-law who had divorced after forty years. All I knew was I could no longer continue to live a life in misery pretending to be happy. I thought about my childhood and how much my parents argued and fought and the days that I wished my mother would leave and take us away from the loud arguing, cussing, carrying on and fighting. Oddly enough, although these two women carried such heaviness, I could see the strength that it took for them to finally walk away. I was able to find the inner strength to recognize that I had to be the example to my children. I learned that I needed to break the cycle of pretending that the fairytale of remaining in a marriage and pretending to be happy was causing more harm, hurt and pain. My fear was not being strong enough to deal with the emotional pressure. After all, I had watched both of these women fall into significant depression and other challenges.

It became clear that certain ties I was connected with had to be broken for me to embrace positive change through divorce and stepping outside the norm.

Church

Some of us grew up during times where what mattered most was how we looked and less about how we felt. The message seemed to be that if we prayed our troubles away, they would just leave. I learned to pray at an early age and with each experience in life. How could I attend church every Sunday, yet feel so empty? Even though I was active in the church during this time, I could not tell my pastor.

As life continued to happen around me, church was always my foundation and place of refuge. However, I had to learn to master my skills and knowledge to remind myself of who I was because those around me were hurting while praising. Determination to change the narrative became my focus. The "Fake it to you make it" was not going to be me.

A level of resilience through adversity was all around me. When I looked at the faces of those in my family, I had to use their experiences and stories as my steppingstones towards growth.

How was I able to cultivate resilience and positive mindset shifts:

- Strong faith in God and truly trusting his promise.

- Understanding that my assignment and the need for change was bigger than myself.
- Knowing that I was responsible to children who were deserving of a better future and the ability to embrace every opportunity.
- Understanding the importance of education as a non-negotiable. Knowing that a solid education could not be taken away.
- Positive affirmations and truly meditating daily on myself and believing in God is what shifted my mindset and patterns of thought. It took recognizing that what others might say was not my story. It took believing that all things are possible as long as I remain faithful.
- Not accepting less than what we should.
- Adjusting my attitude and understanding that hard work takes discipline.
- Determination and believing in my own abilities

Setting and achieving goals beyond ancestral limitations:

- Examining how others in my family overcame their circumstances.
- Examining the decisions that were made and pushing myself more.
- Writing every dream, desire and goal down.
- Looking back at accomplishments and successful goals.
- Remaining focused on achieving better and not repeating cycles and patterns of the past.

Celebrating successes on the journey of breaking curses

History will motivate us to places that we could never imagine. Through the process of self-discovery and understanding myself, I learned that positive change starts with accepting myself and my uniqueness. It's about loving and embracing all of my differences and using them to my advantage. It was amazing when I realized that my thoughts of being viewed as a stranger in a foreign land were actually a blessing in disguise. It helped me to understand that it is never about who people say that I am, but who I believe in my heart I am. It allows for a fresh perspective and the opportunity to learn and grow in ways you never thought possible.

Imagining positive change may seem daunting when you feel like you don't belong, but it is possible. It starts with changing your mindset and seeing yourself as a valuable and important individual. It's about finding your own sense of belonging, whether it's in a new community or within yourself.

I share every WIN with my family!

In the end, embracing positive change means being open to new experiences, being willing to let go of the past, and being confident in your ability to adapt and thrive. It's not always easy, but it is worth it. And through this journey, I have learned that I am capable of so much more than I ever thought possible.

Utilize this space to journal and reflect. What are your thoughts after reading this chapter?

CHAPTER 9
Guarding Against Recurrence
Dr. Lashonda Wofford

At this point, the coauthors have taken you on a ride through their own personal journeys of 'Breaking the Chains to Liberate their lineage from Generational Curses and or Patterns.' Now I would ask that you continue the ride as we journey through the various strategies for preventing the resurgence of generational curses.

On these journeys, we arrive at a pivotal point in our exploration. In this chapter, I will delve deep into the critical aspects of maintaining vigilance and self-awareness to ensure that the hard-fought battle against generational curses continues to bear fruit. It's not just about breaking free from the chains, but about ensuring the legacy of healing and empowerment persist, enriching not just our lives but the lives of future generations. This chapter is a beacon of hope, guiding you on how to guard and nurture the legacy you've worked so hard to create.

As a child I was always so proud to be a Brewington. Everywhere I went, people knew who we were. They didn't necessarily know me and the cousins under me, but they knew my mom and all her sisters. In my eyes, my family unit was perfect, and we loved and respected each other. We were taught to stick together no matter what.

This mentality was the same one that caused me to be loyal to my family regardless of how they treated me and or what they did. It caused me to overlook many things that I felt weren't right or didn't make me feel warm and fuzzy inside. It caused me to make up excuses in my mind regarding their behavior and 'give them passes' just because they were family. I wanted them to like, love, respect and be proud of me. I never wanted to *not* live up to the Brewington name.

I never knew my family was plagued with generational curses and or generational dysfunctional patterns. It wasn't until I became an adult that I found out that my family was no different than other families I had seen. The difference was those families didn't try to hide their issues: they fought and cussed each other out in public and well, we just knew how to dress the issues up in the finest clothes, jewelry etc., so that everything appeared perfect. For years I thought we were a close-knit family, only to find out the family I had known my entire life was the total opposite. We were taught to hide everything and not talk about anything. Unknowingly, unresolved issues and secrets that were in the family for years created a ripple effect on my cousins before my generation and the generations behind me.

There was a spirit of competition, jealousy, and envy that caused backbiting, backstabbing and division among the family and it broke my heart. Let's not forget about the cliques. It puzzles me on how quickly the family can create a united front and stand wrong together, however the same united front is needed to come together and resolve the issues that's deeply rooted from generations now, but no one really wants to deal with them.

All I ever wanted was to be loved for real in private the way I appeared to be loved in the public eye.

Although we can't force others to join us on this journey of healing, self-awareness and breaking generational curses and or patterns we have the power to decide how we change the narrative for our lives and the future generations. I decided I was no longer willing to be an active participant in the destruction of my children and grandchildren. I refused to pass down generational trauma and dysfunction. When I do that, I am passing love, generational wealth, great memories, deeds and legacy to my children and grandkids.

With that being said, I had to be willing to unlearn everything that I had been taught and adapt healthier habits to incorporate into my life, my children, and the lives of my grandchildren.

Here are some important strategies I implemented and still practice on my journey of Breaking Generational Curses and Patterns.

1. **Vigilance as a Lifelong Commitment:** Breaking generational curses is a profound accomplishment, but it's important to understand that the journey doesn't end here. Vigilance is an ongoing commitment to safeguarding your newfound freedom.

    - The importance of vigilance – It is crucial to stay alert and proactive even after breaking generational curses.
    - Recognizing potential triggers – Identifying situations or circumstances that could threaten the resurgence of old patterns.
    - Regular Self Assessments - Developing a habit of self-reflection and self-awareness to stay on course.

2. **Passing Down a Legacy of Healing and Empowerment:** Breaking free from generational curses is not just a personal victory, it's an opportunity to create a legacy of healing and empowerment for your family and future generations.

    - Teaching resilience: Strategies for instilling in your children and grandchildren, ensuring they can face life's challenges with strength and grace.
    - Fostering a culture of open communication: The importance of creating a family environment

where open dialogue about struggles and victories is encouraged.
- Leading by example: How your own journey can inspire and motivate your loved ones to seek healing and empowerment.
- Sharing wisdom: Passing down knowledge and strategies you've gained to equip the next generation.

3. **The Power of Story and Traditions:** Stories and healthy traditions have the remarkable ability to preserve legacy and impart valuable lessons.

   - Family narratives: Sharing stories of your family's journey can inspire and educate younger generations.
   - Creating family traditions: Establishing rituals and practices that reinforce the values of healing, empowerment, and resilience.
   - Using storytelling as a healing tool: How storytelling can be therapeutic and help in the healing process.

4. **The Role of Education and Mentorship:** Education and mentorship play a pivotal role in passing down a legacy of healing and empowerment.

   - Educational opportunities: Providing access to education and learning experiences for your family.
   - Mentorship within the family: Nurturing mentorship relationships to guide and support younger family members.
   - Connecting with external mentors: Encouraging your family to seek mentorship and learn beyond the family circle.

5. **Building a supportive community sustaining a legacy of healing and empowerment often extends beyond the family unit.**

    - Community involvement: Engaging with the community can reinforce the value you've cultivated within your family.
    - Supportive networks: Creating and maintaining connections with like-minded individuals and organizations.

6. **Maintaining Progress:** The process of breaking generational curses is often gradual and requires consistent conscious effort. If you stop being proactive, you risk undoing the progress you've made. It's essential to continue reinforcing positive changes.

7. **Safeguarding Future Generations:** Your journey to breaking generational curses and or patterns isn't just about yourself; it's also about setting a positive example for future generations. Staying vigilant ensures that you pass on a legacy of healing and empowerment rather than a legacy of destructive and dysfunctional patterns.

8. **Coping with Life's Challenges:** Life is filled with ups and downs. Staying alert and proactive equips you with the skills and mindset needed to navigate challenges effectively. It ensures that you have tools to cope with adversity without restoring to old, harmful patterns.

9. **Personal Growth:** Continual self-awareness and personal growth are keys to a fulfilling and purposeful life. By staying alert and proactive, you continue to

evolve as a person, continually improving your well-being and other relationships.

10. **Inspiring others:** Your commitment to maintaining positive change can serve as an inspiration to others in your family and your community. When people see that generational curses and or patterns can be broken and that the transformation can be sustained, it motivates them to embark on the same or similar journeys.

11. **Enhancing Emotional Health:** Staying proactive and maintaining good mental and emotional well-being is essential for long-term emotional health. It helps you manage stress, anxiety, and a host of other emotional challenges that may be contributing factors in the generational curses and or patterns in the first place.

12. **Creating a Supportive Environment:** Being vigilant allows you to create and maintain a supportive environment within the family, which is very important. Open communication, trust and understanding thrive best when you actively work to prevent the recurrence of destructive patterns.

13. **Fulfilling Personal Goals:** Your journey to break generational curses and or patterns more than likely will involve setting personal goals, aspirations and setting boundaries. Staying proactive ensures that you continue to make progress in a forward motion towards the goals that will ultimately lead to a more fulfilling life.

14. **Taking Responsibility:** Part of breaking generational curses involves taking responsibility for your own actions and choices. Staying alert and proactive are

ways of demonstrating ongoing accountability for your well-being and the well-being of those around you.

It's important to remember that staying alert and proactive after breaking generational curses is essential for maintaining progress, safeguarding future generations, and living a fulfilling, purposeful life. It allows you to navigate life's challenges with resilience and inspires positive change in your family and community. It is an ongoing commitment and lots of work to your own healing and empowerment and a testament to your strength and determination.

It's time to do the work! Self-Assessment Tool (Framework)

1. Understanding Generational Patterns

- Identifying Patterns: List any repeated behaviors or circumstances in your family that you perceive as negative. (e.g., financial struggles, relationship issues)

- Family History: Reflect on your family's history. Are there any known events that might have contributed to these patterns?

- Personal Impact: How do you think these patterns have influenced your family's dynamics and individual members?

2. Personal Reflection

- Self-Analysis: In what ways have you noticed these patterns manifesting in your own life?

- Emotional Response: Describe your feelings when you encounter these patterns in your life. (e.g., frustration, acceptance)

- Desire for Change: What motivates you to break these cycles? Consider your goals and aspirations that are hindered by these patterns.

3. Breaking the Cycle

- Setting Goals: Define clear, achievable goals for yourself to overcome these patterns. (e.g., saving money, healthy relationships)

- Action Steps: List specific actions you can take to reach these goals. (e.g., creating a budget, seeking relationship counseling)

- Seeking Support: Identify people or resources that can support you in this journey (e.g., trusted friends, support groups).

4. Maintaining Change

- Monitoring Progress: How will you track your progress towards breaking these patterns?

- Coping Strategies: What strategies will you use to deal with setbacks or challenges?

- Self-Care: Outline practices that you will adopt for your mental and emotional well-being.

5. Resources and Support

- Professional Help: Provide contacts for therapists or counselors specializing in family dynamics.

- Educational Materials: Suggest books, websites, or articles that offer insight into breaking generational patterns.

- Community Support: List support groups, forums, or community organizations that focus on similar issues.

This framework provides a comprehensive approach to understanding and breaking generational patterns. Remember, the journey to breaking these cycles is deeply personal and can vary greatly from one individual to

another. Professional guidance is recommended, especially for complex or deeply ingrained issues.

The work continues...

Framework for recognizing potential triggers when breaking generational curses or patterns is crucial for managing and overcoming these challenges effectively. This framework can be divided into several key areas:

1. Awareness of Historical Patterns

- Family History Review: Understand and document the history of generational patterns in your family. Look for repeated behaviors or circumstances.

- Identify Key Triggers in Family History: Note any specific events, behaviors, or emotions that seem to trigger the negative patterns.

2. Personal Trigger Identification

- Self-Reflection: Regularly reflect on times when you feel most stressed, anxious, or upset. What are the common themes or situations?

- Journaling: Keep a daily or weekly journal to track your emotional states and the events leading up to them. This can help identify personal triggers.

3. Emotional Response and Behavior Analysis

- Emotional Patterns: Pay attention to recurring emotional responses you have. Are there specific situations or discussions that consistently evoke strong emotions?

- Behavioral Responses: Observe your behaviors in response to potential triggers. Do you notice any patterns that mirror those you are trying to break?

4. External Influences

- Social Interactions: Be aware of how interactions with family members or others may trigger certain behaviors or emotions.

- Environmental Factors: Consider if certain places, times of the year, or cultural practices have any influence on triggering these patterns.

5. Coping Strategies

- Developing Coping Mechanisms: Learn and practice healthy coping strategies such as mindfulness, deep breathing, or speaking with a trusted friend or counselor.

- Avoidance vs. Addressing: Understand when it's healthier to avoid certain triggers and when it's necessary to confront and work through them.

6. Seeking Support

- Professional Assistance: Consider seeking help from a therapist or counselor, especially for complex or deep-rooted triggers.

- Support Groups: Engage with groups or communities who are also working through breaking generational patterns. Sharing experiences can provide insights and support.

7. Regular Review and Adaptation

- Continuous Learning: As you grow and change, your triggers may also evolve. Regularly review and update your understanding of your triggers.

- Adaptation of Strategies: Be open to changing your coping strategies as you gain more insight into your triggers and responses.

This framework is intended to guide individuals in recognizing and managing the triggers associated with generational curses or patterns. It's important to approach this process with patience and self-compassion, as it involves deep personal exploration and gradual change.

The work continues...

Journaling can be a powerful tool for introspection and progress in breaking generational curses or patterns. Here are some prompts designed to guide reflection and foster personal growth in this context:

1. Identify the Patterns:

Describe a recurring pattern in your family that you want to change.

_____
_____
_____
_____
_____
_____
_____
_____
_____
_____
_____
_____
_____
_____
_____
_____
_____

Reflect on how this pattern has been passed down through generations.

_____
_____
_____
_____
_____
_____
_____
_____
_____
_____
_____
_____
_____
_____
_____
_____
_____
_____
_____
_____
_____
_____

2. Understanding Personal Impact:

How have these generational patterns affected your personal life choices and behaviors?

_____
_____
_____
_____
_____
_____
_____
_____
_____
_____
_____
_____
_____
_____
_____
_____
_____
_____

Write about a time when you noticed yourself repeating a family pattern. How did you feel?

3. Exploring Root Causes:

What do you think are the root causes of these patterns in your family?

_____
_____
_____
_____
_____
_____
_____
_____
_____
_____
_____
_____
_____
_____
_____
_____
_____
_____

Consider any historical or cultural factors that might have contributed to these patterns.

4. Setting Intentions for Change:

What specific aspects of these generational patterns do you want to change?

_____
_____
_____
_____
_____
_____
_____
_____
_____
_____
_____
_____
_____
_____
_____
_____
_____
_____
_____
_____

Write about your ideal future where these patterns are no longer present. What does it look like?

_____
_____
_____
_____
_____
_____
_____
_____
_____
_____
_____
_____
_____
_____
_____
_____
_____
_____
_____
_____

5. Identifying Triggers and Responses:

Reflect on situations that trigger behaviors or emotions related to these patterns.

_____
_____
_____
_____
_____
_____
_____
_____
_____
_____
_____
_____
_____
_____
_____
_____
_____
_____
_____

How do you typically respond to these triggers? How would you like to respond differently?

_____

_____

_____

_____

_____

_____

_____

_____

_____

_____

_____

_____

_____

_____

_____

_____

_____

_____

_____

_____

6. Exploring Feelings and Emotions:

What emotions do you experience when you think about these generational patterns?

_____
_____
_____
_____
_____
_____
_____
_____
_____
_____
_____
_____
_____
_____
_____
_____
_____
_____

Write about any guilt, shame, or resistance you feel in breaking these patterns.

_____

_____

_____

_____

_____

_____

_____

_____

_____

_____

_____

_____

_____

_____

_____

_____

_____

_____

7. Envisioning Success:

Describe what success in breaking these patterns would mean for you.

_____
_____
_____
_____
_____
_____
_____
_____
_____
_____
_____
_____
_____
_____
_____
_____
_____
_____
_____
_____

How will your life be different when you've broken these generational patterns?

_____
_____
_____
_____
_____
_____
_____
_____
_____
_____
_____
_____
_____
_____
_____
_____
_____
_____
_____
_____
_____

8. Seeking Support and Resources:

What kind of support do you need to break these patterns? Who can you turn to?

_____
_____
_____
_____
_____
_____
_____
_____
_____
_____
_____
_____
_____
_____
_____
_____
_____
_____
_____

Are there any books, articles, or other resources that could help you understand and address these patterns?

9. Reflecting on Progress:

Write about the progress you've made so far in breaking these patterns.

_____
_____
_____
_____
_____
_____
_____
_____
_____
_____
_____
_____
_____
_____
_____
_____
_____
_____
_____

What challenges have you faced, and how have you overcome them?

_____
_____
_____
_____
_____
_____
_____
_____
_____
_____
_____
_____
_____
_____
_____
_____
_____
_____
_____
_____
_____

10. Practicing Gratitude and Acknowledgement:

What strengths do you possess that will help you break these patterns?

_____
_____
_____
_____
_____
_____
_____
_____
_____
_____
_____
_____
_____
_____
_____
_____
_____
_____
_____
_____

Express gratitude towards yourself for the efforts you're making to initiate change.

These prompts are designed to facilitate deep reflection and encourage proactive steps towards breaking harmful generational patterns. Regular journaling using these prompts can be a valuable part of the journey towards personal growth and change.

As I conclude this masterpiece on breaking generational curses and liberating our lineage, it's vital to reflect on the profound journey we've embarked upon. This path isn't just about changing ourselves; it's a transformative process that rewrites the story of our families, both past and future. By courageously confronting and healing the wounds of our ancestors, we are not only liberating ourselves but also paving a new path for the generations to come.

Remember, the process of breaking generational curses is not linear. It involves moments of profound insight and challenging periods of struggle. Along this journey, we may encounter deep-seated fears, unresolved traumas, and unexpected obstacles. Yet, with each step forward, we are peeling back layers of old patterns, creating room for healing and growth.

This chapter of your life is about more than just breaking away from the past; it's about building a new future. It's about recognizing that you are the pivot point – a bridge between the past and a new legacy. Each decision you make, each pattern you break, and each curse you lift is a testament to your strength and the love for your lineage.

As you move forward, carry with you the lessons and insights from this chapter. Hold close the understanding that change starts within you. Remember the power of self-reflection, the importance of seeking support, and the strength that comes from vulnerability. Cherish the small victories along your journey, for they are the foundation of profound transformation.

Embrace your role as a Chain Breaker in your lineage. The work you do now is a profound act of love, a gift that will reverberate through generations. You are not just breaking curses; you are weaving a new tapestry of hope, resilience, and empowerment for yourself and for those who will follow.

As this chapter closes, take a moment to acknowledge your courage and commitment. The path to liberating our lineage is a sacred one, filled with both challenges and triumphs. But remember, every step you take is a step towards a brighter, healthier future for you and your loved ones. You are the architect of a new legacy, one built on the foundations of awareness, healing, and unconditional love. As you move forward on this path, always remember no matter what obstacles you face, keep going and never give up. This liberation is not about you alone. When you feel like giving up, think about your children, their children and the future generations to come. We owe it to ourselves and the generations coming behind us. Think about our ancestors and those that came before us and how proud they would be to know that the chains that have held us captive have finally been broken. I am the Chain Breaker for my family, and I will bring liberation to my entire bloodline.

This process of breaking generational curses is akin to tending a garden. Just as a gardener must identify and remove weeds to allow the garden to flourish, so must we identify and uproot the harmful patterns ingrained in our lineage. This work is meticulous and demanding, but it is also profoundly rewarding. As we clear away the old, toxic patterns, we make space for new, healthier ways of being to take root and grow.

In doing this work, we are not just rewriting our own stories; we are also honoring our ancestors. Many of them carried these curses not out of choice, but out of circumstance. In recognizing and healing these patterns, we acknowledge their struggles and offer them a form of retroactive solace and understanding. We carry their stories, but we also have the power to transform the narrative and end cycles of pain and limitation.

Moreover, this journey is an act of profound hope. It is a declaration that the future can be different from the past. Each moment of self-awareness, every small act of change, is a rebellion against the destiny that these generational curses tried to dictate. By choosing healing, we are choosing to believe in the possibility of a better tomorrow, not just for ourselves but for those who come after us.

As you continue on this path, be gentle with yourself. Change of this magnitude does not happen overnight. There will be moments of doubt and setbacks. In these moments, remember why you started. Recall the vision of a liberated lineage, free from the shackles of the past. Draw strength from this vision and from the community of others who walk this path alongside you.

Remember, you are not alone on this journey. Across the world, there are many embarking on similar paths of healing and transformation. Draw inspiration from their stories, share your own, and build a network of support. Together, there is immense strength and wisdom to be found.

As we close this chapter, let's look forward with hope and determination. The work of breaking generational curses is one of the most significant challenges we can undertake, but it is also one of the most rewarding. It's a journey of becoming, a process of continuous evolution and growth.

Carry forward the lessons learned, the insights gained, and the strength you've mustered. Continue to nurture the seeds of change you've planted. With patience, care, and persistence, you will see them bloom into a legacy of freedom, health, and prosperity—a true liberation of your lineage.

I pray this book will be a milestone in your journey, a reminder of how far you've come and a beacon of light for the path ahead. As you turn this page, step forward with confidence and courage, knowing that you are creating a new narrative, one filled with hope, healing, and endless possibilities.

Acknowledgements

With the deepest gratitude, we acknowledge the unwavering spirit and sacrifice of those who came before us. Your battles were not fought in vain; through each challenge and every tear, you built a foundation of strength and resilience that we stand upon today.

We recognize the immense courage it took to confront and overcome the shadows of past generations—breaking cycles of trauma, pain, and limitation. Your determination has not only shaped our present but has illuminated a path for the future, allowing us to pursue dreams unburdened by the chains of the past.

Thank you for your prayers, your perseverance, and your profound love that have guided us toward liberation and healing. Your legacy is not marked by the struggles you faced but by the victories you secured and the hope you instilled in us all.

As we move forward, we carry with us the lessons of endurance and faith you imparted, committed to nurturing and expanding the freedom you fought so hard to achieve. We are forever grateful and promise to honor your legacy by living with intention, courage, and an unwavering commitment to continue what you have started.

This acknowledgment is but a small token of our immense appreciation for your sacrifices and your vision. Thank you for everything.

The Chain Breakers

About the Authors

Dr. Frances Ann Bailey

Born and raised on Eastern Shore of Virginia, Dr. Frances Ann Bailey is a Jesus lover, servant of Christ, an ordained Minister, International Amazon Best-Selling Author, Podcast Host, TEDx Speaker, wife, mother, philanthropist, and an Award-Winning Certified Coach and Certified Christian Counselor.

Also known as the "Purpose Zeal Coach", Dr. Bailey is the CEO of Frances Bailey Enterprises, LLC, the Founder/President of the nonprofit organization Red Door Empowerment, Chancellor of the school Purpose Zeal Academy and the Dean of the Purpose Zeal School of the Great Commission Bible College & Seminary.

Frances has her Associate's in Administrative Support Technology, Bachelor of Science in Criminal Justice with a specialization in CJ management, a Master's in Public Administration, Doctorate in Leadership and a PhD in Business Administration and Entrepreneurship. She also has her Master's in Christian Humanities and Doctorate in Theology from the School of the Great Commission Bible College.

Frances seeks to help women who were once like herself to overcome life's obstacles, break free from bondage, and recover from life setbacks to keep their zeal for purpose. as a Christian Counselor, she also provides spiritual support and guidance based on a Christian prospective to strengthen their relationship with Christ and other personal relationships. Frances exemplifies this by consistently walking in her calling by producing books, birthing a podcast, certifying others to become coaches, business mentorship and professional development programs.

Frances' expertise, testimonies, and wisdom has taken her before great individuals. She been featured on WESR Shore Daily News radio station, the Eastern Shore Post newspaper, Voyage ATL Magazine, the international Walden University Alumni magazine, Glambitious Magazine, Today's Purpose Woman magazine, VIP Global Magazine, Nigeria Woman.NG magazine Sheen Magazine, WoMELLE Magazine and so many more. She has had exclusive interviews and featured on FOX 34, CBS 016, and NBC 21. She was also featured on FOX 34 as

"Top Entrepreneurs You Should Know." She was recently awarded the Presidential Lifetime Achievement Award by the President of the United States for her commitment to leadership and her community and was crowned 2022-2023 Mrs. Virginia (1st runner up for Ms. US). She has also recently been crowned 2023-2024 Mrs. North America - International Woman of Achievement while also being named Mother of the Year for the State of Virginia. Frances was recently honored in London, United Kingdom, with the Wise Woman Life's Turn Around Award and helping those unselfishly to thrive in the Kingdom of God. For all that God has done, She says, "To God be all the Glory."

Willie McCrimmon, Jr.

Apostle Willie McCrimmon Jr, is a 46-year-old Man-of-God out of Pittsboro, North Carolina. One who has ministered for nearly 21 years now and has been a shepherd over God's flock for nearly the same amount of time. Apostle McCrimmon was called, nurtured, taught, and pushed under the leadership of Apostle Jace Cox.

After hearing from God, and accepting His mandate, the Lord led Apostle McCrimmon out of Zion to become the founder of a life-changing ministry called Deliverance Through Christ Outreach Ministries. One church in two locations. Through his obedience to God's work, the Lord has blessed Apostle McCrimmon's hands to heal, deliver, and set free many wounded, broken-hearted and abandoned people across the nation. From various preaching, teaching, prophetic encounters, in and outside of the church the Lord blessed his voice to speak through the radio as well as having his own Christian TV show entitled "Turning Back To God!" Apostle McCrimmon has been blessed with the opportunity to minister in England and has been asked numerous times to minister in India.

Through his TV show, God has used this man of thunder to win souls for the Kingdom; for some time now states, regions, and across the seas; God has put his hands on him with one thing in mind and that is setting the captive free.

Apostle McCrimmon's unique, powerful, and prophetic voice will be one that you will not forget nor regret. Get ready for God's gatekeeper, spirit, insight, and voice while you receive your deliverance.

Dr. Rashia N. Barbee

About Rashia... *"And we know that all things work together for good to them that love God, to them who are the called according to His purpose," Romans 8:28.* This is the favorite scripture of Pastor Rashia N. Barbee, for she has witnessed this verse come alive in her life, time and time again. On August 29,

1979, Pastor Rashia NeCole Barbee was born to the Reverend Dwight Barbee and the late Mrs. Ella Barbee. She is the oldest living grandchild of Ms. Clara L. Wilson. She attended the Chatham County School System and is a 1997 graduate of Northwood High School, Pittsboro, North Carolina. In addition, she has received her Associate's of Arts in Business Administration and her Bachelors of Science degree in Business Administration and Management from the University of Phoenix. She earned her Master's in Leadership at Pfeiffer University in August 2019. Further, Pastor Barbee is a licensed cosmetologist, entrepreneur, CEO and Founder of the Arise Den, LLC and The Arise Insurance Group, a motivational speaker, mentor, author, and pastor.

Pastor Barbee is the proud mother of four handsome boys, Jeremiah, Jamir, Josiah, and Jahaziel. Pastor Barbee was elevated to the pastorate in October 2018 and served as the pastor of Liberty Praise Center under the covering of The Liberty Connection with Apostle Jace L. Cox until 2021. She birthed Arise Nations Assembly, Inc. in the first quarter of 2022 and is simply focused on souls arising to be saved, healed, and delivered. She has a powerful anointing to preach, pray, praise, and provide words of love and encouragement for this present age. Pastor Barbee has birthed the Daughters of Liberty and Love, Travailing Lady Ministries, Esther's Army, and Arise Women Ministries. Pastor Barbee's ministry encourages all to use their power of travail to birth out destiny and not abort it. Pastor Barbee has an all-inclusive ministry that nurtures young girls, heals adult women, speaks men out of dry places, and propels young men to walk as true young warriors for God.

The boldness that Pastor Barbee possesses allows her to walk with authority like the Judge Deborah and persevere like Queen Esther. This handmaiden of God is a consecrated vessel, fit for the Master's use and has no other desire but to please

God. She is prepared in the Gospel and in April 2024, she will earn her Doctorate in Christian Theology. She is always striving to move as a woman after God's own heart.

ShaQuandra Dawson

Shaquandra Dawson is a 28-year-old wife and mother. She is originally from North Carolina but currently lives in the Jacksonville Florida area. Her children are 9 and 2. She also has a 1-year-old fur baby. Her children are the greatest joys of her life, and she loves them dearly.

She has a career in nursing as an RN, which she enjoys. She obtained a BSN degree from Fayetteville State University. She's currently working on obtaining a master's degree from Duke University to become a Family Nurse Practitioner and aspires to become a provider taking care of those in underserved areas.

Though she doesn't have much free time these days, when she does get it she enjoys reading, going out in nature, and just spending time with her family. She has a passion for caring for others during some of the hardest times of their lives, such as when they are facing poor health and sickness. She enjoys teaching and helping others on their healing journey to reach their best selves.

Travis Wofford

Travis Wofford is a multifaceted businessman. He works in multiple fields of industry including healthcare and technology. He is the Co-Founder of Wofford and Williams Inc, the parent company to his many entrepreneurial endeavors. He is President and CFO of Akins Helping Hands, a company that provides healthcare resources to those in need. He is also a Mapping Consultant for Voxel Mapping and Tech Mahindra, aiding the development of technical innovations that we all use every day.

Travis is also a certified Life Coach and Life Recover Coach. He has also added bestselling author to his list with his latest book project 'Love, Business and Marriage.'

Travis grew up in Pittsboro, North Carolina. He graduated from Northwood High School in his hometown, and continued his education at Guilford Tech in Greensboro, North Carolina. He now resides in Hope Mills, North Carolina with his devoted wife and family.

Traveling and learning about new cultures are some of his greatest interests. He loves the thrill of riding motorcycles. And on a regular day, you will find him listening to music and spending time with his family.

Travis hopes to uplift and serve the black male community by mentoring at risk youth within the community and beyond. He feels it is important to have open discourse among men in the black community. His YouTube Channel, The Average Man, serves as a platform for men to come together and discuss topics affecting them in today's society.

Travis is an accomplished professional, but still strives to do more. He is a bestselling author and is building a successful media & entertainment company. He works diligently to continue growing each of his businesses. It is his goal for Akins Helping Hands to continue growing and providing excellent, quality care to those in need.

Travis feels it is important to create jobs that help the black community improve economically. He wants to pave the way for others to be successful. He also feels a personal mission to build generational wealth for his family.

His skills are what make all this possible. Travis is a technophile and well-versed in IT, machine maintenance, and numerical operations. His foresight is one of his strongest qualities. He works well under pressure and has the ability to assess and harness the strengths and skills of others. He is a natural leader and uses every opportunity to teach those around him. With these talents, Travis will continue to grow in business and help those around him succeed.

Dawanna Alexander

Dawanna Alexander is the CEO and Founder of Lady Shannel Coaching & Consulting LLC and CEO of DSA Scentsy. Dawanna is an Accredited & Certificated Life Recovery Coach.

Through many trials and tribulations, Dawanna has gained strength and developed a passion to help others bounce back from life's setbacks. Her passion for helping and serving others doesn't end there. Her current role as a CST II with UNC Hospital allows Dawanna to walk in her purpose and do what she loves to do.

Dawanna feels that motivating and encouraging others brings new meaning to life as she loves to push others to their NEXT LEVEL through her unique coaching programs.

Dawanna is a dedicated Women of God (WOG), wife and mother. She is a proud member of Deliverance Through Christ Outreach Ministry located in Pittsboro, North Carolina. Dawanna is also a proud member of the best Christian organization on this side of heaven, Sigma Tau Sigma Sorority (Incorporated Federally Registered and Trademarked). She takes pride in being a Sigma Woman and loves to spend time with her Sorors.

Aside from this, she is very family-oriented, and loves spending time with family and friends. Most importantly, she is a true WOG who loves the Lord.

"Life has taught me that I may bend but I will not break. I shall not be defeated."

Connect with Dawanna on Social Media through Facebook and Instagram at Lady Shannel Coaching & Consulting, LLC. DSA Scentsy.

Nichole Shoffner

Nichole Shoffner is a North Carolina native, who also calls Washington DC her second home due to her living in the nation's capital for twenty years, who now resides back in her home state. She is currently a program supervisor at a top pharmaceutical company where she enjoys motivating her agents to grow and succeed in their careers.

She is a daughter and a sister; a mother of two and a grandmother of one; as well as an aunt to her nine nieces and nephews whom she loves to spend time with and spoil as much as she can.

Nichole recently received her nationally and internationally mental health specialist coach certification through All Bets On Me Academy and has planned to endure in starting her own business called Serenity Solutions, through which her business she plans to assist with youth and single mothers who may need assistance or resources to thrive in the community.

Shani'ya Faucette

Shani'ya Faucette is a new author and is known for her willingness to help. With a background in counseling and as a behavior therapist, she has developed an understanding of human psychology. Shani'ya's writing shows the sensitivity, compassion, and empathy that she houses for her audience.

Her writing invites readers to unleash the best versions of themselves and reflects passion to explore all aspects of human identity in its entirety. Through her writing, Shani'ya hopes to inspire others to embark on healing, create intentional conversations, and to have lasting positive impact on the hearts and minds of readers.

Dr. Karon Graves

Early on in her professional career, Dr. Karon Graves centered her energy around working with vulnerable populations within the community. Her passion to serve others began in Massachusetts (1991), in Early Childhood Education where she served in various capacities from teacher to educational resource coordinator. She continued to expand her career and spent some years working with developmentally disabled adults.

In 2002 Dr. Graves began her career in Child Welfare providing direct services to children and families with the State of Connecticut Department of Children and Families. During her tenure with the State of Connecticut Department of Children and Families, she served in many social work and supervisor roles for over thirteen years of service. In 2015, after relocating to North Carolina, she continued her work in child welfare where she continues to serve with over twenty years of service overall.

Dr. Graves is an adoptive parent after fostering a relative placement for six years in Massachusetts. During her time serving as a relative foster parent, she became a CASA-certified Guardian ad Litem in an effort to advocate for timely permanency outcomes for children in the foster care system.

Dr. Karon Graves is a graduate of Springfield College where she earned both a Bachelor of Science and a Master's of Science in Human Services. She holds a PhD in Chrisitan Leadership from the Purpose Zeal Bible College & Seminary. Her additional educational experience includes doctoral studies in counseling. Dr. Graves is a Certified Recovery Life Coach and holds several other certifications related to Early Childhood Education.

Dr. Graves is the founder of Push Towards Purpose Supportive Services, LLC, which is a recovery life coaching company founded on the belief that everyone deserves the support and guidance needed to achieve their desired goals. They strive to help individuals who have been impacted by trauma and life stress-related challenges to make positive changes in their lives. Their experienced team of professionals provide the best possible service to their clients, ensuring that they are well-supported and have the tools and resources to work towards their goals. She is passionate about helping people find their purpose and take the necessary steps to achieve success. She committed to helping our clients create the life they desire and deserve. Dr. Graves has published a Coaching Workbook to assist others along their journey.

Dr. Graves if the founder and owner of Push Tax Solutions where she provides tax preparation, education, and business coaching.

With over twenty years dedicated to the field of Human Services, Dr. Graves works and volunteers in her community. As she continues to be of service to others to implement change. She has been active in various communities in multiple states because of her care, compassion, and dedication to humanity.

Most importantly, Dr. Graves loves the Lord. At an early age, she gave her life to the Lord and was baptized at the age of eight-years-old. Her passion for God, church, and family has been her guiding light. She has served in several ministries over the years from Sunday School Teacher, Praise and Worship Leader, Usher, Choir member, Women's Day Chair, Executive Director of The Food Bank, and Trustee.

Dr. Lashonda Wofford

Dr. Lashonda Wofford is a Woman of God, wife, a mother, a sister, a grandmother, a friend, and a proven CEO. She has founded and built several successful organizations, including The Affirmation Collection and L&S Consulting Group. Wofford And Williams Inc dba Akins Helping Hands which is a seven-figure Home Care Business based out of Hope Mills, North Carolina. She is also the proud owner of Empower Her Legacy; Purposeful Collective. She is a community advocate and personal development partner who encourages all to bet on themselves through her All Bets on Me platform on Facebook. She's the founder and host of the international podcast called The All Bets on Me Podcast. Her newest business ventures are The All Bets on Me Academy, and Akins Global Diagnostics Laboratory Solutions, both launched in the Spring of 2024.

Through various pains and struggles, Dr. Wofford has learned to bet on herself and accomplish her goals despite adversities. She is a successful businesswoman of color who breaks the ceiling and creates tables for other women to have the same opportunities as she has. Some of Lashonda's noteworthy accomplishments are serving in the following roles: internationally and nationally accredited certified instructor partnered with Purpose Zeal Academy, certified executive leadership coach, certified life recovery coach, certified mental health counselor, certified transformation coach and a certified Art Therapy Practitioner.

She is also a seven-times best-selling author for the anthology project, Blessed Not Broken, Volume I, her solo project Pain Equals Purpose, anthology Igniting Your Purpose, 90 Days of Biblical Affirmations for Christian Women in Business and Ministry, Love Business Marriage and Becoming Her and Marketplace Mogul, all of which can be purchased at www.drlashondawofford.com.

She is the recipient of the 2022 ACHI Award for Public Service. Recipient of the 2023 Trailblazer Award from the School of the Great Commission Theological Seminary. Recipient of the 2023 Author of the Year for her solo book project Pain Equals Purpose from the InspireU Network

Awards and the recipient of the 2023 Power and Grace Leader Award for Coach of The Year. Dr. Wofford received The President's Lifetime Achievement Award in 2024 and was also selected for inclusion in The Nationwide Registries Women of Distinction 2024 Honors Edition.

Dr. Wofford has been nominated for multiple awards including but not limited to The God Made Millionaire Award and the DWAP Award in three categories Woman To Watch, Game Changer and the Author Of Influence.

Dr. Wofford and her husband are proud members of Mt. Zion AME Zion Church located in Eastover, North Carolina. Dr. Wofford takes pride in also being a member of the Lock4Love Sisterhood based out of Sanford, North Carolina.

You can connect with Dr. Wofford on:

Facebook:
https://www.facebook.com/lashonda.wofford.72mibextid=LQQJ4d

All Bets On Me:
https://www.facebook.com/groups/1124117394775943/?

All Things Coaching:
https://www.facebook.com/groups/1097641824230355/?

All Bets On Me Academy:
https://dr-lashonda-wofford-s-school.teachable.com/

Milton Keynes UK
Ingram Content Group UK Ltd.
UKHW050901300824
447605UK00006B/166